Rotherham Workhouse

Rotherham Workhouse

Margaret Drinkall

Front cover, top The walls of Rotherham workhouse (courtesy of RALS).

Front cover, bottom High Street, 1905-09 (courtesy of RALS).

Back cover Women and babies, Aston, 1901-20 (courtesy of RALS).

First published 2009

The History Press
The Mill, Brimscombe Port
Stroud, Gloucestershire, GL5 2QG
www.thehistorypress.co.uk

British Library Cataloguing in Publication Data.
A catalogue record for this book is available from the British Library.

ISBN 978 0 7524 5290 6

Typesetting and origination by The History Press
Printed in Great Britain

Contents

	Acknowledgements	6
	Preface	7
one	The Old Poor Laws and Life in the Rotherham Workhouse	9
two	The Board of Guardians	23
three	The Medical Officers of Health	36
four	The Workhouse Chaplain	44
five	The Master and Matron	56
six	Teachers and Education in the Workhouse	63
seven	Giving Birth and Children in the Workhouse	68
eight	Lunatics and Imbeciles	76
nine	Mismanagement and Allegations at the Workhouse	83
	Appendix: Some of the Workhouse Paupers Mentioned in the Guardians' Minutes	103
	Bibliography	125

Acknowledgements

Many people have been instrumental in helping me write this book and to them I extend my grateful thanks. Firstly, for the patience and forbearing of my two sons, Steve and Chris: as always, with my love. I would also like to thank the staff of the Rotherham Archives and Local Studies (RALS) Department for all their help, which has been invaluable. Thanks also to Tim Brannen, the Illustrations Assistant at RMBC, for his work on the images for the book, almost all of which were supplied by the Rotherham Archives and Local Studies Service, with the exception of the reproduction of the photograph of the Crowson family which is by courtesy of Mrs Irene Crowson. I would also like to extend my grateful thanks to Geoff and Sue Booker (Rotherham Web), David Speck (Hull in Print), Tom de Wit (Westbury Manor Museum), George P. Landow (Victorian Web), Chris Hobbs (*Sheffield Star*) and Geoffrey Rivett (NHS History) for permission to use extracts in the book.

I also want to make special mention of friends Chris and Fiona Ruane, Julie Darrington and Ruth Peattie, all of whom offered encouragement and spurred me on. But most of all to Cate Ludlow at The History Press whose unfailing support has been instrumental in the production of this book. Also from The History Press, my sincere thanks to Nicola Guy, David Lewis and Helen Bradbury.

For anyone who wishes to learn more about my experience of the publishing process or information about future books, see the website at margaretdrinkall.co.uk.

Almost last, but not least, I want to thank the Rotherham Board of Guardians, who took the time to ensure that their decision making was recorded, and the several clerks to the Guardians who painstakingly copied these decisions of the Guardians' meetings into the minute book. But I am most grateful of all to the inhabitants of the Rotherham workhouse, of whom very little is known. Their lives within the workhouse and their reasons for entering it remain unrecorded. All that is certain is that despite the Guardians' and the Poor Law Commissioners' view that most people who entered the Rotherham workhouse were generally idle and shiftless, reality proves that people would only enter the workhouse as a last resort when everything else had been tried and tested. People would, and did, starve to death before entering its walls. It is to these people that I extend my grateful thanks; hopefully I am able to shine a small light onto their existences within that terrible place.

Preface

The introduction of the Poor Law Act of 1834, followed closely by the Poor Law Amendment Act of the same year, was a revolution in the way that legislation looked at the needs of the poor. The intention was that with the introduction of these Acts no able-bodied pauper would be given outdoor relief; therefore they would be forced to enter the workhouse. The Poor Law Commissioners thought this would simultaneously reduce the amount of relief paid out and as a bonus remove the poor out of sight. There is plenty of evidence within the Rotherham Board of Guardians' minutes to illustrate that the workhouse system did not work, not because of the Guardians themselves as administrators of relief, but simply because of the large number of inmates who were unable to work or move on. Inmates such as children, people with physical and learning disabilities and the elderly men and women resulted in the workhouse gradually filling up with paupers and the costs of relief becoming astronomical.

The records of Rotherham workhouse were kept by a variety of clerks and the handwriting differs throughout the records. The writing is sometimes very hard to decipher and the lack of punctuation occasionally makes reading difficult, but any mistakes which are made here are my own. In reference to money I have used the old system of pounds, shillings and pence (i.e. 20s refers to twenty shillings, and £1 5s 6d refers to one pound, five shillings and sixpence). I have used as many names as I am able to under the Freedom of Information Act and urge anyone who feels that I am discussing a relative of theirs to remember that the stigma of poverty was endemic in Victorian society and the fact that at least a record of their relatives' lives remains. It should not be seen as a disgrace. Written before the days of political correctness, the terms used in the minutes are thankfully not acceptable today. However, for accuracy I will use the terms as written, with many apologies if I offend readers, which is not my intention.

I decided to close my study in 1902 as this was the year where the Rotherham workhouse began to take hospital status, reducing the fear for many poor of the town. Nevertheless, the alarm of going into the hospital replaced the fear of the workhouse for many years to come, due in some part to the original use of many of these buildings in the West Riding of Yorkshire. The lives of the paupers were so different to those of the people on the Board of Guardians who made the laws, but I do believe that the Rotherham Guardians were honestly trying to make the lives of their charges easier; they truly felt themselves to be the 'Guardians' of Rotherham's poor and needy.

one

The Old Poor Laws and Life in the Rotherham Workhouse

The old Poor Laws were developed out of a growing sense of a parish's responsibility towards its poor. Prior to the Reformation, monasteries and abbeys had mainly dealt charitably with the elderly and sick of the parish. They also gave relief to tramps and vagrants passing through the towns who had no visible means of support. Since the closure of the monasteries by Henry VIII in 1536, townships such as Rotherham took responsibility for their own poor and sick. Overseers of the parish would undertake this task by drawing up lists of ratepayers within the town, collecting taxes from their properties and distributing it to the poor and sick in the form of relief. These overseers would be ratepayers and respectable men of the town such as vicars or churchwardens, who would give up their time freely to undertake such tasks. Rotherham also had a group of town trustees who administered relief to the poor, known as the Feoffees of the Common Lands. They bought and sold land, and the revenues so raised were used to provide relief to the poor of the town.

After the plague years, when labour was short, men would go to other parts of the country to find work and support their families. But if they became sick or unemployed and had to claim relief, this would lead to the problem of 'settlement' (where the pauper had to prove that they had a claim to live or be 'settled' within that parish). Naturally, overseers, and later Guardians, were reluctant to pay for paupers that were not of their own parish, and throughout the Board of Guardians' minutes there are many queries about settlement. People could only claim this by rights of property, having lived in the area for more than a year – or, if they were female, by settling in their husband's parish. Without any of these rights, newcomers to the town could be brought before the local Bench if they deemed them 'likely to be chargeable to the parish poor rates'. Any person wishing to move out of their own area would need a letter from the Justice of the Peace or risk punishment in the stocks as a vagabond.

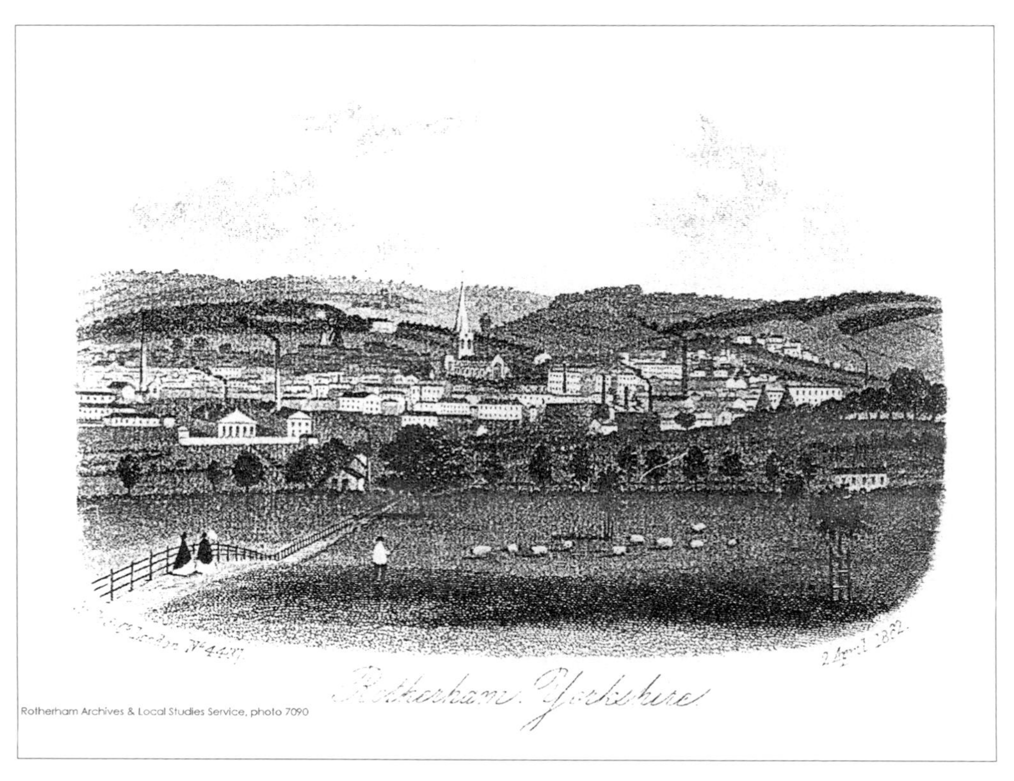

Rotherham Archives & Local Studies Service, photo 7090

Rotherham in 1862.

Parish paupers who were able to prove their 'settlement' and were given relief were often required to wear something to distinguish them from the more 'respectable poor' who were not on relief. As John Guest shows in his *Historic Notices of Rotherham*, stigmatisation towards the poor in Rotherham resulted in them being forced to wear a particular badge indicating their status, which was a legal procedure resulting from the William III Act which stated that 'every person receiving parish relief shall wear upon the right shoulder of the outer garments a badge either in red or blue cloth consisting of a large Roman P preceded with the first letter of the name of the place where the person lives' (i.e. paupers in Rotherham would have RP inscribed on the badge).

The Poor Law Amendment Act came into force in 1834. It encouraged parishes to join together to build large union workhouses to replace the many scattered small workhouses throughout the parishes. These small workhouses were found in the small townships of Kimberworth, Greasbrough, Rawmarsh Laughton and Rotherham. But most importantly, the Act ensured that no relief would be supplied to able-bodied paupers outside of the large union workhouse. It was felt that by building these larger workhouses the administrative tasks of relieving the poor would be simplified. The reality, however, was that bigger workhouses simply meant bigger costs of relief.

The model guidelines were developed by the Poor Law Commissioners, a group of people responsible to the government to oversee the Board of Guardians. These Commissioners were later called the Poor Law Board (and later still, the Local Government Board). The guidelines specified that a group of respectable townspeople be elected onto the Board of Guardians yearly, to meet on a regular basis and take on the responsibility for the relief of the poor of Rotherham. The Guardians were empowered to elect workhouse officials to aid them in their task. This board would be led by local landowners – in Rotherham's case, the Earl Fitzwilliam and the Earl of Effingham.

The Rotherham Guardians and the Poor Law Commissioners believed that strict reductions of the lists of paupers and controlling the payment of rates would inevitably result in savings for the ratepayers. However, periods of escalating unemployment, frequent epidemics and increases in the numbers of paupers who were termed 'imbeciles' and 'lunatics' led to massive overcrowding in the house. This resulted in estimated costs rising to unprecedented levels. Prior to the new Act, elderly or sick paupers would be helped out by neighbours in their community, who well understood the cyclical nature of poverty. Often only a few shillings would be needed. However, the huge numbers of paupers in these institutions meant significant outlays in relief. All this was yet to happen when, in July 1837, the Rotherham Guardians drew up their lists of paupers and decided what was to be done until the union workhouse could be built in the town.

The Poor Law Commissioners had developed the Consolidated General Order of 1847 which laid down the way in which Guardians would be elected and the roles of the workhouse officers. It became a Bible with which many of the local Board of Guardians would develop their role. The order indicated the classification of the paupers into seven categories upon admittance to the union workhouses. They were:

Men infirm through age or any other cause

Able-bodied males over fifteen

Boys between the ages of seven and fifteen

Women infirm through age or any other cause

Able-bodied females over fifteen

Girls between seven and fifteen

Children under seven

The walls of Rotherham workhouse.

The 5th Earl, Charles William Wentworth Fitzwilliam.

The 4th Earl of Effingham in 1907.

The walls of Rotherham workhouse.

Slums (now demolished).

The cost of the relief of the poor and the cost of building the union workhouse was to be paid for by the ratepayers of the town of Rotherham. Many of the houses of the town were in a poor condition and were of no rateable value, and so the relief would have to be paid by people with rateable property of over £5 per year. Property valuation lists were drawn up with the help of the overseers of the poor, and relieving officers were to be appointed. Calls (or rates) would be made on the value of properties within each parish, some being wealthier than others. On 24 July 1837, the Guardians resolved to 'provide the union with the funds estimated to be required to defray the current expenses of the union'. They resolved that the calls on the several parishes shall be 10 per cent on the declared averages of each, and demanded that the 'several accounts shall be paid to the treasurer on or before the 7th August next'. Orders were accordingly signed directing the parish officers of the several parishes to pay the following sums which were listed in the minutes:

Parish	10 per cent of call	Total call
Rotherham	£103 16s	£1,038
Brinsworth	£9 4s	£92
Catcliffe	£4 18s	£49
Dalton	£8 14s	£87
Greasbrough	£53	£530
Kimberworth	£79 2s	£791
Orgreave	£4 4s	£42
Tinsley	£17 18s	£179
Aston cum Oughton	£18 8s	£184
Bramley	£10 8s	£104
Brampton En Le Morthern	£5 16s	£58
Treeton	£19 18s	£199
Ulley	£4 16s	£48
Brampton Bierlow	£39 12s	£396
Swinton	£32 4s	£322
Wath upon Dearne	£38 16s	£388
Wentworth	£39 4s	£392
Hooton Levitt	£6	£60
Maltby	£25 16s	£258
Hooton Roberts	£12 10s	£125
Laughton En Le Morthern	£28 18s	£289
Ravenfield	£10 12s	£106
Rawmarsh	£50	£500
Thrybergh	£11 12s	£116
Whiston	£39 2s	£391
Wickersley	£15 12s	£156
Beighton	£29 8s	£294
Total	£719 8s	£7,194

There was much resentment from the parishes at having to pay these calls, but with the backing of the Poor Law Commissioners the Guardians' demands were very clear. They gave specific dates by which these amounts had to be paid, and districts that did not fulfil their obligations were prosecuted. There are many instances quoted in the minutes of the different parishes requesting extra time to pay these calls. In September 1837 the Guardians were told by the clerk that several parishes had not paid to the treasurer the amounts due to them: they were told that 'unless payments were paid in full on or before the 17th instant, legal proceedings would be taken against them'.

Once the large union workhouse at Rotherham had opened (in around June 1838), the able-bodied poor of the town were not given relief but instead issued with tickets of entry to the workhouse. These tickets would be given by the relieving officers who were stationed in the different districts. Later these tickets would also be given by police constables. Many of the instructions of the Poor Law Commissioners held

The walls of Rotherham workhouse.

the view that poverty amongst able-bodied men and women was a direct result of their own idleness. *The Sixth Report of the Poor Law Commissioners 1840, England and Wales plus Ireland* (which you may read for yourself at www.institutions.org.uk/poor_law_unions/unmarried_mothers.htm) shows that their view of the purpose of the workhouses was very clear:

> The sole object of the workhouses is to give relief to the destitute poor in such a manner as shall satisfy their necessary wants, without making pauperism attractive, or otherwise injuring the industrious classes. The workhouse is not intended to serve any penal or remuneratory purpose: and it ought not to be used for punishing the dissolute.

Nevertheless, the main function of the workhouse was as a deterrent to the idle poor, and in this it succeeded. Some of the newspaper reports indicate the dire poverty to which people of Rotherham and other towns were subject – and reveal how many of the paupers would rather starve than approach the relieving officers for help. Such a case was reported in the *Rotherham Advertiser* on the 6 February 1897, under the by-line 'How the Poor Live'; it involved the death of a widow, Mary Anne Branch, aged fifty-one, at the workhouse. The medical officer, Dr Alfred Robinson, had attended to her when she was admitted on the 22 February, and found that she was in a state of collapse and unable to give an account of herself. He treated her for starvation and neglect. It was reported that she earned her living by singing and begging and had lived in the many lodging houses of the town. These houses were notorious slums, as were the houses of the poor, and there were many dark courts where sunlight could rarely be seen for any length of time. In the summer, Mary Anne would stay out all night rather than pay even the smallest lodging-house fees, and by the time she was admitted she was much emaciated. She died on the 29th. The jury returned a verdict of death from natural causes accelerated by privation and neglect. The coroner stated that if she had gone to the workhouse earlier she would have been in a better state than she had been prior to her death. He added that, 'people of that class rather than submit to a bit of control and confinement in the workhouse will for the sake of liberty go out, having no where to live and nothing to live upon. Hundreds do this sort of thing'.

From now on even the entry process into the workhouse was seen as demeaning, and paupers were treated as a lower form of life. Immediately upon admission, the new inmates were separated from their families, men from wives and children from their parents. Their clothing was removed, disinfected and stored until they left the workhouse. Paupers were admitted into the receiving wards where they were searched and washed and were required to put on workhouse clothing. This was institutionalised clothing which was functional and basic. Studying the lists of provision for clothing, which changed very little over the years, the standard wear seemed to consist of 'men's and boy's worsted jackets', 'trowsers' and shirts. For women, materials such as gingham and checks were bought, possibly worn as aprons over dresses of unbleached calico. The usual footwear for men and boys were hob-nailed boots; women and girls wore shoes. On admission to the workhouse the pauper's hair would be cropped by the

Rotherham Archives & Local Studies Service, photo142

Slums (now demolished).

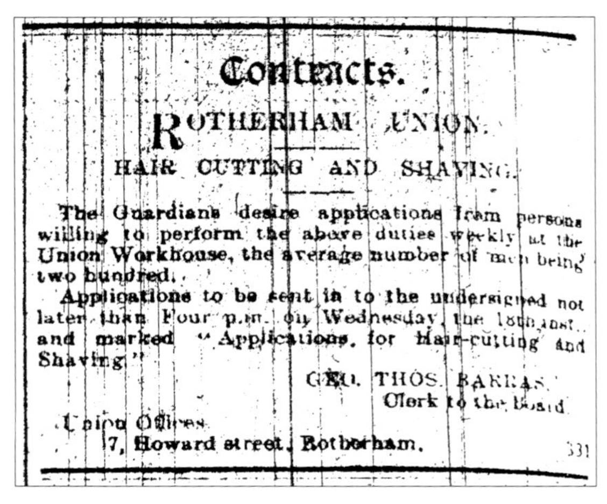

Contracts.

ROTHERHAM UNION.

HAIR CUTTING AND SHAVING.

The Guardians desire applications from persons willing to perform the above duties weekly at the Union Workhouse, the average number of men being two hundred.

Applications to be sent in to the undersigned not later than Four p.m. on Wednesday, the 18th inst., and marked "Applications for Hair-cutting and Shaving."

GEO. THOS. BARRAS,
Clerk to the Board

Union Offices,
7, Howard street, Rotherham.

331

Above Application for post of workhouse barber.

ROTHERHAM UNION.

CONTRACTS FOR PROVISIONS, CLOTHING, &c.

Persons desirous of Contracting with the Guardians of the above Union for the supply of any of the Articles undermentioned, to the expiration of the Quarter ending on the 25th day of September next, are requested to deliver Sealed Tenders at the Board Room, at the Town Hall, in Rotherham, on MONDAY, the 21st day of JUNE instant, at Ten o'clock in the Morning.

BREAD, Good Seconds, or Household, at per 4lb. loaf.

FLOUR, best Superfine, at per stone.

FLOUR, best Baker's Fine, at per stone.

BEEF, consisting of Legs, Flanks, Fore Offal, Marrow Bones, and Suet, at per stone.

MUTTON, all Joints, except Legs, at per stone.

OATMEAL, at per stone. CHEESE, at per lb.

YELLOW SOAP, at per stone. SOFT SOAP, at per firkin.

SALT, at per stone. SODA, at per stone.

Black TEA, COFFEE, Raw SUGAR, RICE, BLACK PEPPER, MUSTARD, GINGER, TREACLE, DIPPED CANDLES, STARCH, and POWDER BLUE, each at per lb.

Men's and Boys' Strong FUSTIAN COATS, WAISTCOATS, and TROUSERS, each.

Men's, Women's, and Children's SHOES, at per pair.

FLANNEL, at per yard.

Grey CALICO, at per yard. White CALICO, at per yard.

Scotch SHEETING, at per yard. WOOLSEY, at per yard.

GINGHAM, at per yard. Scouring FLANNEL, at per yard.

WORSTED, for knitting, at per lb.

HANDKERCHIEFS, at per dozen.

RUGS, BLANKETS, SHEETING, and Materials for Bed and Bolster Cases.

Men's, Women's, Boy's and Girl's Strong SHOES, at per pair.

COALS, at per ton.

BRUSHES, at per dozen, according to size.

Samples of the above Articles, except Meat, must be produced with the Tenders.

The several Articles Contracted for, will be required to be delivered at such times, and in such quantities, at the Union Workhouse, in Rotherham, as the Board may from time to time direct.

The Persons whose Tenders may be accepted, will be required to enter into Bonds (with a Surety or Sureties, if considered necessary) for the due performance of the Contract.

By Order,
JOHN BARRAS,
Clerk to the Board of Guardians.

Rotherham, 14th June, 1858.

Left Tenders for clothing.

workhouse barber, the same haircut given to men and women. Men would also be shaved by the barber on a regular basis as no sharp implements such as scissors or razors were allowed in the workhouse. Applications for tenders for the barber were advertised in the local newspaper. The paupers would then be examined by the medical officer of health. If they showed any sign of illness they would be admitted into the hospital; otherwise they would be directed into the segregated day rooms and given work to do. This completed the hated initiation into the walls of Rotherham workhouse.

The regime in the workhouse was purposely hard and meant to daunt even the toughest pauper. The usual timetable show that the inmates would rise at 6 a.m. from March to September (7 a.m. from September to March), have half an hour for breakfast from 6.30–7 a.m. before going to work (which would start at 7 a.m. and finish at 6 p.m. with an hour's break for lunch). Supper would be from 6–7 p.m. and bedtime was 8 p.m.

No talking was allowed during mealtimes and any bad behaviour was entered into the master's punishment book. Naturally, able-bodied inmates of the workhouse were expected to work in return for their accommodation or maintenance, and a stone yard was provided for this purpose. The Guardians of Rotherham received advice from the Poor Law Commission on the amount of hours which these paupers would work in return for being maintained in the workhouse. The amount of scales of relief would vary throughout the minutes and many discussions took place on this subject. In January 1854 the Guardians resolved that the scale for 'all poor applying for relief on the grounds of want of employment should be set to work at the workhouse for 9-10 hours per day'. The work for an able-bodied man would consist of breaking stones or cinders and chopping up railway sleepers for firewood. Older inmates and children would pick oakum. The work for able-bodied females would be more of the domestic variety such as working in the workhouse laundry, cooking in the kitchens, cleaning or sewing.

The cost of each inmate's relief was expected to be paid by family members out of the workhouse. The costs could be enforced by law, and wages were attached when necessary. Many of the inmates were deserted wives and their cases were

Walls of the Rotherham workhouse.

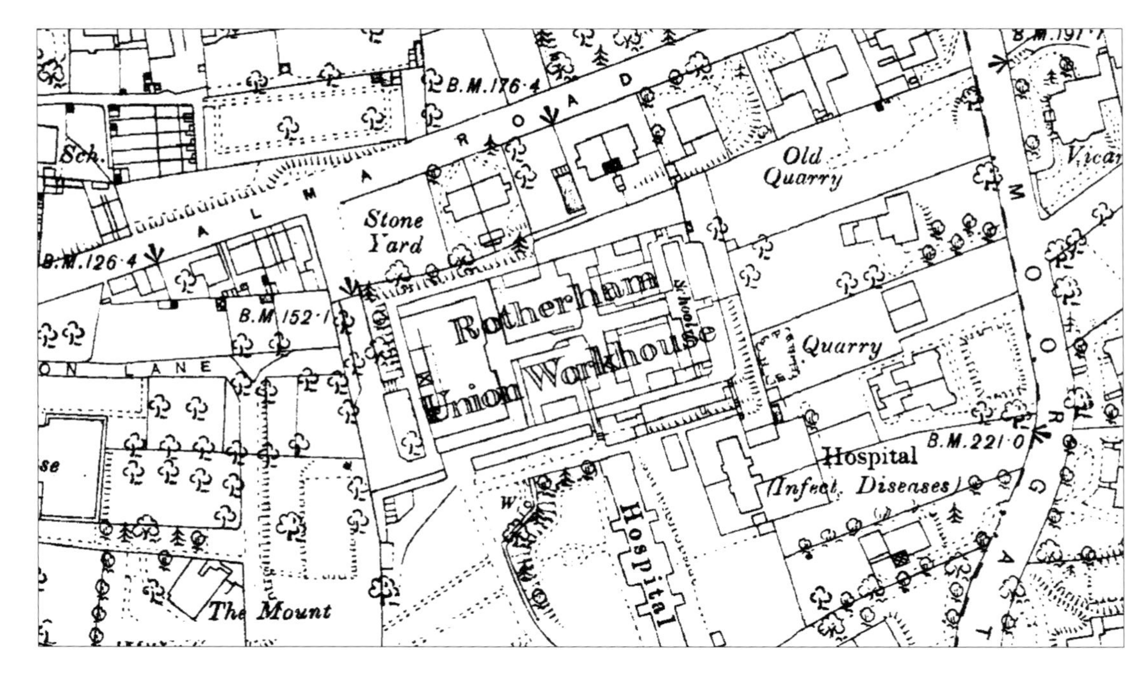

Map of Rotherham Workhouse 1888 (Ref 289-11).

Rotherham Archives & Local Studies Service, photo 15868

The courthouse, College Square, 1905-10.

A DISORDERLY PAUPER SENT TO PRISON.

At the Rotherham Police Court, on Thursday, before the Mayor (Councillor Steddart), and other magistrates, John Burns, an inmate of the Rotherham Workhouse, appeared in the dock on a charge of disorderly conduct and threatening Mr W. D. Walton, the head master of the workhouse, on the 26th July. —Mr G. T. Barras, clerk to the Board of Guardians, prosecuted, and said that was a case in which the Guardians have specially asked him to appear because it was a rather bad case. For a period of eighteen months the prisoner had been doing scale work, and during the greater portion of this time he was supposed to have been suffering from some lameness of the leg. On the 16th July, in order to test the prisoner he was admitted into the house, ten days later he was examined by the medical officer, who reported that he was able to break stones. During the whole of the time he had been in the house he had acted in a very disorderly manner, had threatened the master, and had refused to do his work. He had also made use of profane language. The offence with which he was now charged was that he refused to observe the regulations of the house. He (Mr Barras) would call Mr Walton, the workhouse master, who would prove that he took off his coat and threatened to assault him, and made use of bad language.—In reply to the bench, Mr Barras said scale work was one ton a day. While he was doing scale work he lived out of the house.—Mr Walton produced the admission and discharge book, and said on the 16th July, the prisoner was admitted into the house with his four children. On the 26th July he was examined by the medical officer, who certified that he was able to break cinders. On the 2nd August, when witness was going to Sheffield, he spoke to the prisoner and told him to get on with his work. He replied that he would not be ordered about, and threatened to "drive his —— pick into him."—Prisoner denied this, and said Mr Walton called him an idle man.—Mr Barker, porter of the workhouse, said he had to deal with the men who did the work. The prisoner was an idle man, and when he was put to work with the other men, he would neither work himself nor let the other men perform their duty. He had been before the Guardians, and had insulted them while they had to send for witness to eject the prisoner, who afterwards said, "They wanted me to break stones. They can take a horse to the water to drink, but they could not make him drink," meaning that the Guardians could not make him work. On the 25th July, the prisoner said he should not do the work, and made use of obscene language towards the Guardians. For nearly a week he had only broken 1 ton 4cwt. of stones, in which time he should have broken 5 tons. He had had every opportunity of seeking work out of the house.—Prisoner now said he had worked 28 years in Rotherham, and about two years ago he got lamed.—Mr Walton remarked that the prisoner had said he had gone to the workhouse to pass his time, and he would not work neither for him nor the Guardians. He had paid rates for many years.—Prisoner: I am willing to do my best, and I can do no more.—The Mayor said the prisoner would be committed to prison for 14 days, and the Bench hoped it would be a lesson to him. They had power to double the term of imprisonment next time, and if he came before them again, in all probability he would be committed for one month. He thought prisoner would find breaking cinders at the workhouse very much better than going to gaol.—Prisoner: I can only do my best.

John Burns sentenced to fourteen days in prison.

heard in the local courthouse in College Square. In July 1880 Thomas Blackburn, described as a nail maker of Rotherham, was accused of leaving his wife and three children chargeable to the union to the sum of 5s 4d. He was found in Leicester and brought back to Rotherham. It was reported in the local newspaper that this was the third time he had deserted his wife and family to look for work. The Guardians suggested that if he had been unable to find work he would have been given work at the workhouse. The prisoner said the he wanted 'better paying work than would be paid at the workhouse'. For the crime of deserting his family in order to obtain employment for them all resulted in his being committed to the House of Correction for one month. The work at the workhouse was very unpopular and many inmates would refuse to do the tasks assigned to them. Such a case was that of John Burns, who refused to do the work and threatened the master in August 1887. He was taken before the magistrate and sentenced to fourteen days; the magistrate added that if he came before him again for the same crime he would be sentenced to one month's imprisonment.

Sometimes the Guardians were empowered by law to seize bequests which could be used for the maintenance of a pauper who had been sent to the local asylum and who was the responsibility of the Rotherham Guardians. In February 1893, the clerk informed the Guardians that he had been corresponding with solicitors Messrs Saunders, Nicholson and Reedes in reference to the claim for maintenance of Betsy Jane Sayles, a pauper lunatic from Rotherham who was now an inmate at the asylum at Wadsley. The clerk informed the Guardians that she had inherited £56 6s 9d under the will of Mrs Harriett Sayles, deceased, which the Guardians felt should be used for her maintenance. The clerk was ordered to receive the money and hand it over to the relieving officer for payment into the bank to defray the cost of her relief.

The administration of the workhouse and the developing system of relief demanded by the Poor Law Acts was a massive task for anyone to take on. The people who would take on this responsibility were a group of local businessmen and the two earls. They had to find and buy the land for the workhouse, arrange a loan for the building, develop the system of calls on the parishes and administer the cost of relief. This group of businessmen were the Rotherham Board of Guardians.

two

The Board of Guardians

On Monday 3 July 1837 a group of people met in the imposing courthouse in Rotherham town centre, a building which no longer exists, to elect a Board of Guardians of the Poor. Unanimously elected as *ex officio* Guardian was the local landowner Earl Fitzwilliam; as chairman of the board and to deputise in his absence, John Fullerton Esquire; and as vice chair, the Reverend Doctor Milner. These *ex officio* Guardians were people who were automatically elected due to their status and position in the town. In Rotherham the Guardians included two Earl Fitzwilliams: the 5th Earl served until his death in October 1857, followed by his son, William Thomas Spencer, the 6th Earl, from 1857 to his death in 1902.

The board's first task was to decide how many Guardians would be needed, and it was agreed that one Guardian would be appointed for each of the twenty-seven parishes (apart from Rotherham and Kimberworth, whose population was larger; it was therefore more appropriate that two Guardians would be appointed for those districts). The very first Rotherham Board of Guardians were:

Guardians name	Parish	Guardians name	Parish
John Aldred	Rotherham	John Jackson	Brampton Bierlow
Edward Pagden	Rotherham	Thomas Bingley	Swinton
Francis Parker	Brinsworth	William Carr	Wath
William Rawling	Catcliffe	Benjamin Buyram	Wentworth
John Didsbury	Dalton	Revd William Henry Downes	Laughton En Le Morthern
Edward Jackson	Greasbrough	Roger Heywood	Hooton Levitt
Jonathon Bray	Kimberworth	John Horncastle	Maltby
William Glossop	Kimberworth	William Frith	Hooton Robert
John Oxley	Orgreave	Thomas Bosville	Ravenfield
Henry Dyson	Tinsley	James White	Rawmarsh
Francis Moss	Aston	William Whitaker	Thrybergh

Joseph Roberts	Bramley	Revd Walter Shirley	Whiston
John J. Glossop	B. En Le Mor.	Revd John Foster	Wickersley
John Jubb	Beighton	Robert Taylor	Treeton
William Moss	Ulley		

The Guardians agreed at this first meeting that they would meet weekly, on Mondays at 10 a.m., at the old Town Hall, still in existence on Effingham Street. It was further agreed that as soon as the new union workhouse was completed, the Guardians would meet on the first Monday of every month at the union workhouse in the specially build board room. The Guardians resolved that:

> a workhouse for the accommodation of 350 individuals [was] to be built within the union and that the following Gentlemen be appointed a committee to look out for an eligible site and report the same to the board viz: John Fullerton Esq, Revd John Foster, Revd William Henry Downes, John Aldred, Edward Pagden, Francis Parker and Robert Taylor and that such committee meet at 12 o'clock Wednesday next.

It was agreed at the second meeting that a list of paupers belonging to Rotherham, Kimberworth and Greasbrough would be examined and personally visited the following week by the relieving officer (who would report back to the Guardians as to their condition). As a temporary measure until the new workhouse was built, any paupers who were sick or ill would receive out-door relief which could be given in half and half, that is half in money and half in bread.

The Court House, College Square, where the first Board of Guardians met on 3 July 1837.

John Fullerton, Deputy Chair of the Guardians.

John Aldred, Guardian for Rotherham.

Before work on the building could begin, the Rotherham Guardians needed to identify a suitable piece of land on which the workhouse would be built. In October 1837 the building committee reported that a five-acre piece of land had been offered by the Feoffees for £1,000. By May 1838, the clerk was instructed to 'take the necessary steps for obtaining a loan of £6,000 from the Sheffield and Rotherham Bank for the purpose of building the new union workhouse' on an elevated site described as being 'at the bottom of Westgate'; although it is unclear from the minutes when the workhouse was actually finished, a local solicitor was ordered to sell the furniture from the 'old workhouse' by auction in June 1839. Two months later the minutes note that 'the workhouse at Rawmarsh has been given up and the in-door paupers removed to the union workhouse'.

The Poor Law Commissioners' architectural plans for workhouses were intended for them to be large, airy buildings, simultaneously imposing and forbidding. According to such plans Rotherham workhouse was built as a large, three-storey building with unexpectedly elegant chimneys on otherwise very austere walls. Its position in Alma Road would have made a large impact on the town it overlooked and could be seen from many parts of the town. Although there are no remaining plans of the workhouse, local maps indicate a square plan such as that designed by Sampson Kempthorne (I discovered this on Peter Higginbotham's excellent website, www.workhouses.org.uk). His designs would typically show four yards separating the male and female paupers

Above The Assembly rooms at the Old Town Hall, where the Guardians held their meetings.

Left Rotherham Union workhouse.

Right Feoffees' procession, 1951.

Below Westgate, 1906-07.

The austere walls of the Rotherham workhouse.

and boys and girls in a cruciform design (with a central block containing the master and matron's rooms). From these central rooms all the yards could be observed by the master and matron, and anyone coming or going could be seen.

The Rotherham Guardians then turned their attention to the officers of the workhouse system: which officers would live in the workhouse, and which officers would reside in the several parishes. Firstly, they dealt with those officers who would collect the rates and the medical officers of health who would reside in the districts. Initially it had been decided that only one relieving officer was necessary, but this soon proved unworkable. It was decided that, for the purposes of employing relieving officers and medical officers, the town of Rotherham would be divided into seven districts: these would consist of Rotherham, Kimberworth, Wath, Swinton, Maltby, Laughton and Beighton, and each parish would have its own medical officer and relieving officer. The clerk placed advertisements in the local newspapers for these posts and the applications were closely inspected by the Building Committee. It was agreed that the officers would be elected on a yearly basis and each had to reside less than a mile from the districts they were responsible for. Later posts were advertised in the local papers for officers who would reside within the walls of the workhouse – such as the master and matron, the schoolteachers, and at a later date, the workhouse nurses.

The work of the Guardians was to ensure the smooth running of the workhouse and to provide an account of the way the relief was paid. Supplies and provisions were tendered for and contracts signed. For those who did not come up to scratch, penalties had to be paid. The supply of bread to the Rotherham workhouse had been an issue for many years, and discussions were held regarding the provision of a bake house. Despite a couple of attempts, the idea was soon dismissed and the supplies of bread were tendered for once again. In March 1860 the baker, Mr Sales, admitted that potato peelings had been baked in the bread supplied to the Rotherham workhouse and his contract was terminated. Perhaps because of this kind of contamination a rumour held sway that the bread given to the poor was poisoned in an attempt to get rid of pauperism. This rumour was felt to be based in fact and spread throughout the country, fanned by some of the radical national newspapers such as the *Times*. The paupers, however, had a choice: eat it or starve. After March 1873, the Guardians required a bond of £100 for all successful suppliers of goods to the Rotherham workhouse.

The distribution of relief was proving very difficult and expensive for the Guardians and it was soon realised by the Poor Law Commissioners that admitting every able-bodied pauper into the union workhouses was quickly becoming unmanageable. On 13 April 1842, the Outdoor Labour Test Order was issued by them which offered relief in return for the performance of deterrent manual labour for up to ten hours a day, the men remaining during the night in their own homes in the town. The work was usually stone-breaking or wood chopping undertaken in a labour yard attached to the workhouse (and later situated in the town itself) and the Poor Law Commissioners resolved that the relief should be paid in half and half. This kind of work was very unpopular with the paupers, and as we have seen the reality was that people would starve to death rather than to seek any kind of relief. Great lengths would be taken to find work outside before being admitted to

Rotherham Archives & Local Studies Service, photo 468

Alma Road.

the workhouse. The *Rotherham and Masbrough Advertiser* reported that a child was found dead in its mother's arms on the 2 May 1863. The parents were Mr and Mrs Henry James Sirridge, cork cutters from Bristol. They had both been travelling about the country seeking work. On Friday 24 April they had left Doncaster to walk to Rotherham and whilst at Thrybergh the child began to cry and appeared unwell. The mother took it to a farmhouse nearby and asked for a drink for the child. The person solicitously made the child a sop (bread and milk) and the child appeared better and went to sleep. Nevertheless, soon afterwards the mother found the child dead and cold. They were just half a mile away from Rotherham. A verdict of 'death by natural causes' was given by the jury.

As you will see, the Guardians at Rotherham were assiduous in their duties – unlike some workhouses. In August of 1908, ten Guardians had been put on trial from the Mile End workhouse accused of receiving subsidies from contractors in order to deceive the ratepayers. An alderman, a church warden and the former Mayor of Stepney were given terms of imprisonment following a similar scandal in West Ham workhouse in 1907. In Andover the chair to the Guardians, Revd Christopher Dodson, had not visited the workhouse for five years when a scandal broke out about the inmates fighting over the rotting bones for any meat which might be attached. The case was reported avidly by the *Times* newspaper. (You can read more about this at http://victorianweb.org/history/poorlaw/andover.html)

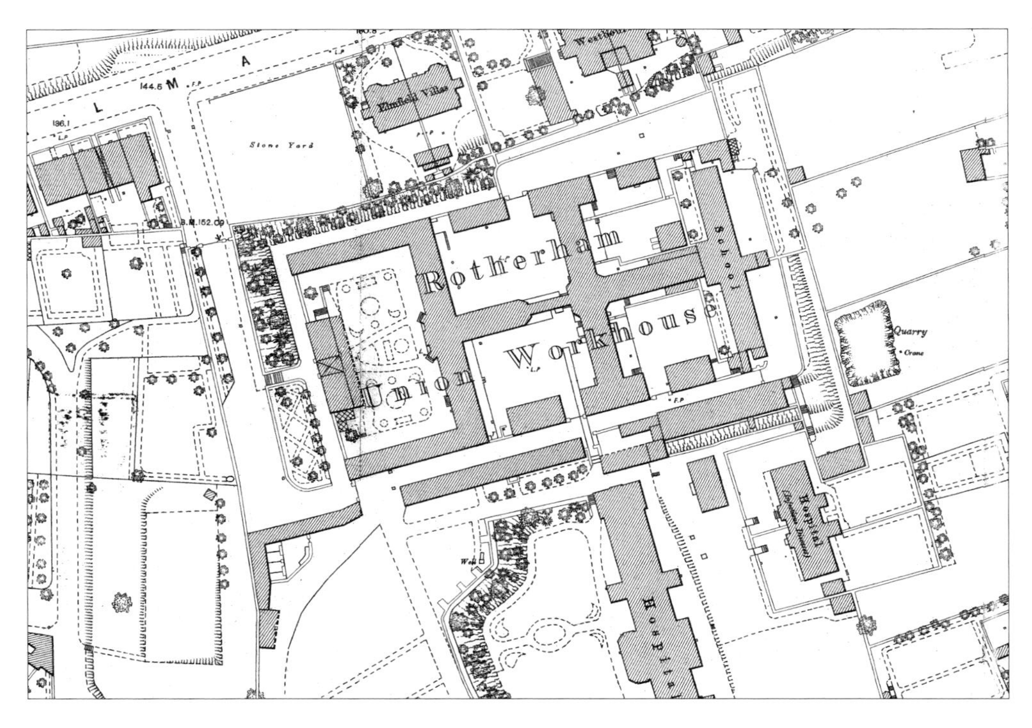

Cruciform shape of the workhouse (Ref 289-11-17).

ROTHERHAM BOARD OF GUARDIANS.

A fortnightly meeting of the Rotherham Board of Guardians was held at the Workhouse, Alma road, Rotherham, on Monday morning. Mr J. Jubb presided, and there were also present Mr W. Blunn (vice-chairman), Alderman Wragg, Messrs. Harrop, Sorsby, Whitworth, Walker, Booth, Parker, Skinner, Huntsman, Cox, Foers, Wells, and Easton.

RELIEF RETURNS.

Return for the week ending August 6.—Workhouse: Number of inmates remaining last week, 306; admitted, 26; discharged, 19; dead, 2; remaining at the end of the week, 311; corresponding week last year, 309; cutaneous eruption cases, 1; opthalmia, 1.........The CLERK (Mr G. T. Barras) reported that last week out relief had been administered to 1957 persons, at a cost of £158 6s. 2d.; while in the corresponding week of last year the number had been 2072, and the cost £169 5s. 7d. Last week 51 tramps had been admitted to the casual ward, as compared with 34 last year.

POOR LAW INSPECTOR'S ANNUAL RETURNS.

The CLERK submitted a report from Mr Kennedy, the Poor Law Inspector, showing that in Rotherham the percentage of pauperism to population in 1886 was 2·7, and this year 3·0; the rate in the pound on the rateable value was 7·1d. this year, and the rate per head was 3·9s. In Barnsley the figures were in 1886, 2·6 and 2·8 in 1887. The rate in the pound was 9·2d.; the rate per head of the population was about the same as in Rotherham. In Sheffield the percentage of pauperism to the population was 4·2, the rate in the pound 1s.; the rate per head of the population was 4s. In Wakefield the percentage of pauperism was 3·2, the rate was 7·7, as against 7·1d., the rate per head 3·1s., or rather more than Rotherham.......The CHAIRMAN remarked that evidently Rotherham stood very well in comparison......Mr WHITWORTH said the figures showed they in Rotherham had nothing to care about.

THE BAKEHOUSE QUESTION.

A deputation had visited the Ecclesall and Fir Vale Workhouses to see the arrangements for baking bread, &c......Mr WELLS spoke favourably of the change proposed in Rotherham......Mr COX said that the cost of baking their own bread in Rotherham would be nearly 4d. per 4lb. loaf. They would have to bake 172 stones, or 600 loaves, and the difference would be about 25s. in favour of baking their own bread, but this would be about exhausted in securing the services of a baker. The cost of the oven would be about £130......Mr WELLS said that the committee unanimously recommended the proposed change ...In the course of some further conversation, Mr COX said that the cost of a second oven would be about £50......On the motion of the CHAIRMAN, seconded by Mr HUNTSMAN, it was resolved that the committee be instructed to get plans for the proposed works.

The Board then sat in committee.

Discussions regarding a bake house at the workhouse.

It was agreed by the Rotherham Guardians that a visiting committee would be formed on 11 April 1842 who would visit the workhouse on a weekly basis and report back to the Guardians with any issues which had arisen. The numbers of Guardians were listed on a rota ensuring that every board meeting day, two Guardians would attend the workhouse throughout the year and inspect the building. Remarks on any issues would be made in the visitor's book kept at the workhouse and the book would be presented to the Guardians at the weekly board meetings. The Board of Guardian's minutes show that by October 1850 the attention of the Guardians was drawn to the 'infrequent attendance of the visiting committee to the workhouse'. It was resolved that the committee would be expected to attend punctiliously on every board day and a new list was drawn up. The Guardians agreed in January 1860 that perhaps a female visiting committee could promote more gentleness in the running of the workhouse. The Ladies Committee were only allowed to visit the inmates of the Rotherham workhouse under very strict observance of the rules which had been suggested by Louisa Twining and were copied into the minutes:

Visitors shall attend the workhouse at hours most convenient to the inmates and officers and shall observe the rules of the workhouse.

Visitors shall abstain from all interference with religious opinions of those who differ from them.

That the workhouse be allotted to the Ladies Visiting Committee in the following manner:

Able-bodied men's ward:	2 visitors	Able-bodied women's ward:	2 visitors
Old men's ward:	1 visitor	Old women's ward:	1 visitor
Boy's school:	1 visitor	Girl's school:	1 visitor
Male infirmary:	2 visitors	Female infirmary:	2 visitors

In truth, the power of the Ladies Visiting Committee would have been very limited as any decisions would have to be sanctioned by the all-male Board of Guardians. Nevertheless, allowing women to enter the workhouse as visitors was seen as a way of softening the regime of the workhouse, though it would be almost another forty years before any women were accepted onto the Rotherham Board of Guardians. The minutes list that in May 1901, the first lady Guardian attended the board. She was Mrs Alice Mary Habershon. The following week she was joined by Miss G. E. Hirst, both from prominent and respectable families of the town. Like the other Guardians, their attendances were consistent and they also elected to sit in on the many committees who reported back to the board on other issues.

The Guardians' minutes were not just confined to matters regarding the administration of the workhouse. Many national as well as local current events of the town were recorded throughout the period of study. Some of the Guardians were at the same time the Lord Mayor of the town, and as such current events would have been relevant to them. Exceptional national deaths were recorded in the minutes (as in May 1882, when expressions of abhorrence and heart-felt condolences were offered at the death of Lord Frederick Cavendish, son of the Duke of Devonshire, who was murdered – along with the Permanent Under Secretary, Thomas Henry Burke – by Irish nationals in Phoenix Park, Dublin).

Further condolences were sent to the Prince and Princess of Wales following the death of their son, the Duke of Clarence, from pneumonia in January 1892. The Prince of Wales had been to Rotherham the previous year when the town showed its patriotism by decking the streets with bunting. A reply was received, and copied into the minutes, from Sir Deighton Grobyn, comptroller and treasurer of the household at Sandringham, conveying to 'members of the Rotherham Board of Guardians the warm thanks of the Prince and Princess of Wales for the Guardians' kind address in condoling with their Royal Highnesses in their deep bereavement'. But nowhere in the minutes are there records of local tragedies which took place in the town. For example, on 6 July 1841, a boat capsized in Masbrough and fifty local people were killed; a boiler explosion at the Midland Iron Works at Masbrough in December 1862 killed nine men.

Royal visit of the Prince of Wales, 1891.

The Guardians are silent on these matters. However, the minutes continued to record many national events, and it appears that increasingly the Guardians were now including the paupers in royal celebrations.

But the largest national celebrations were naturally held in the town, both in 1887 for Queen Victoria's Golden Jubilee and in 1897 for her Diamond Jubilee. Once again, the town's streets were covered in flags and patriotic symbols. Her Majesty Queen Victoria had been on the throne for sixty glorious years, and the Guardians (and many of the inmates) will have not known any other sovereign. One of the Guardians (and Mayor of Rotherham), Alderman Wragg, said that he felt it 'right and proper that the poor of the town should share in the activities of this glorious occasion. He continued that he remembered the Queen's coronation and her marriage, and stated that 'members of the Guardians have sat around this table and have grown grey in dispensing the rates for the relief of the poor.'

Further celebrations were held in 1902 when the town celebrated the return of Rotherham soldiers from the Boer War in South Africa, and once again the town was decorated to hold a procession. The local newspaper reported that the town had shown great rejoicing at the news of the relief of Mafeking, and a Parkgate landlord reportedly hung out bunting in celebration. There were scenes of the wildest excitement and indescribable enthusiasm witnessed in the town.

Left Mayor George Wragg (1887–1888).

Below Boer War celebrations, High Street, 1902.

Equally, the greatest loss which was recorded in the minutes by the Guardians was the death of Queen Victoria in 1901. It was with great sadness, then, that before the Guardians started the business of the workhouse on the 4 February 1901 the chairman referred to 'the Nation's loss by the death of Her Most Gracious and Beloved Queen Victoria'. Alderman Wragg and Mr Blackburn spoke most feelingly and unanimously resolved that the condolences of the Rotherham Board of Guardians be sent to the new king, which was copied into the minutes:

> The Guardians of the Poor of Rotherham Union hereby unanimously place on record their deep sense of the irreparable loss which this Country and Empire have sustained in consequence of the death of Her Most Gracious Majesty, Our Beloved Queen Victoria. The Guardians most respectfully and dutifully convey to His Majesty the King and all the members of the Royal Family their most sincere sympathy and condolences in their sorrow and painful bereavement. We at the same time desire to congratulate His Majesty on his accession to the throne and assure His Majesty of their constant and devoted loyalty.

It truly did seem like the end of an era. A reply was received and recorded in March 1902 from Charles T. Richie of the Home Office, Whitehall thanking the Guardians for 'the loyal and dutiful resolution of the members of the Rotherham Board of Guardians'.

In stories of abuses of the workhouse systems it was alleged that in some workhouses the Boards of Guardians did not attend their meetings regularly and left the day-to-day running of the workhouse to the master and matron. The Guardians of the Wortley workhouse in Sheffield was censured for this in 1841. However, this was not the case in Rotherham. The Guardians held their meeting weekly, and even on Boxing Day of 1853 a meeting was held which was chaired by Earl of Effingham himself. It seems that they took their duties very seriously. Part of those duties would be the election of the workhouse's doctors, the medical officers of health.

three

The Medical Officers of Health

The medical officer of the union workhouse was responsible for the health and the medical needs of the workhouse inmates and its officers. He was also responsible for paupers on out relief, where he would visit them in their own homes and assess their condition. He oversaw the diets of the inmates and the health of mothers and children in the workhouse and he had to report every birth and death. It was agreed from the early Guardians' meetings that the medical officer would not be called out in cases of midwifery except in emergencies. At a time when the mortality rates for women and children in the town was not good, this seems a very harsh decision. Only later, when the general health of mothers and babies improved, did the mortality rates fall. The minutes show that later cases of difficulties in childbirth saw a relaxation in this rule. It was resolved that where the medical officer had to be called upon to assist at a birth, a fee of 15s would be paid, but 'it is not intended that in every case of a poor person be called in, but only in extreme cases'. The medical officer could order 'extras' for any patient in the workhouse hospital or on out relief in the form of extra food, milk or alcohol (a subject of discontent for the ratepayers of the town, as later events will show).

The Guardians instructed that advertisements for the medical officers were to be inserted in the *Doncaster Gazette,* inviting local medical men to submit applications to the Guardians before Monday 10 June 1837. Like other officials of the workhouse, they were to be elected annually. The first men were appointed in July 1837 and requested to commence their duties on the 19 August. The men appointed were:

Mr Joshua Turner	Rotherham	£35 p.a.
Mr Copeland	Kimberworth	£40 p.a.
Mr Wade	Wath	£20 p.a.
Mr R.A. Blytheman	Swinton	£20 p.a.
Mr F.W. Flowe	Maltby	£15 p.a.
Mr Charles Saw	Laughton	£15 p.a.
Mr Nicholson	Beighton	£15 p.a.

Women and babies, Aston, 1901-20.

The low salaries suggest that these early medical officers had their own practice in the different parishes and that the position of union medical officer was seen as a supplementary role. The workhouse medical officer was naturally responsible for all the deaths at the workhouse and this task caused a scandal in the nearby town of Sheffield which was reported in the *Times* for 31 January 1882. Workhouse paupers' bodies which had not been claimed for burial were sent by the medical officer to the nearest teaching hospital for dissection. A destitute Sheffield pauper had previously sent a letter to the editor of the local newspaper outlining the causes of ill health which had brought him and his family to the brink of starvation. A subscription was started for him and, for a while, matters improved, but with no chance of earning a living he was soon reduced to pauperism and was brought into the workhouse in January from his lodging in West Street. He died within minutes of being at the workhouse infirmary and his body was prepared for burial. His wife, following her instincts, asked to see her husband's body (which was in a closed coffin) and found that inside the coffin was another pauper, a man aged seventy-one. Her husband's body was lying on a slab at the local medical school about to be dissected. The matter was investigated by Mr Basil Cane and the fault was found not with the medical officer, but with the man in charge of the 'dead house'. (See www.chrishobbs.com/shefffieldwhs1882.htm)

There are too many medical officers of the Rotherham districts to deal with individually, but some were some real characters. One of these was Dr Junius Hardwick. He served the Guardians from December 1851 to May 1891, a total of forty years. It seems that a year after his appointment the good doctor was proving his worth as he had made the link between the poor water supply and the outbreak of disease. He gave an opinion to the Guardians in August 1852 that the water at the workhouse was the cause of the epidemic of diarrhoea, and requested that samples of water be tested by an analytical chemist, Mr Hayward of Rotherham. Nevertheless, a frequent complaint about Dr Hardwick surfaced for the first time in April 1856 when he was requested to appear before the Guardians to explain why there was such a difference between Rotherham and other neighbouring unions regarding the extras which were being ordered. (These extras were in the form of alcohol, meat or medicine which had been given to the patient to help in the healing processes at the workhouse hospital.) Dr Hardwick was unable to answer: '[He] expressed himself as being unable to give any explanation of the differences in the expenditure between Rotherham and other neighbouring workhouses for stimulants supplied to patients in the hospital.'

Dr Hardwick's duties required him to attend to the paupers in the workhouse on a regular basis (whilst still maintaining his own practice in the town). Although he was highly thought of by the Guardians, he was strongly criticised in the local papers for neglect of a man called Henry Butterfield, who was taken ill in the town and died. It was reported that in May 1863 the deceased man was visiting friends at the Butter Market in Rotherham when he had a fit and collapsed. He was put by the door of the house for some fresh air and his friend ran to the nearest surgery, which was Dr Hardwick's, and asked the doctor to come at once 'as a man was dying'. Dr Hardwick declined as he had other patients to see to, and sent the man to the nearby surgery of Dr Darwin. This doctor attended and tried unsuccessfully to persuade the friends to bring the man (who was now lying in the street) into their house, but for whatever reason they were reluctant to do this. The police inspector, Mr Gillett, arrived, and seeing that the man was very ill indeed, got a cab and took him to the workhouse. He noted the time was 3.20 p.m. when Mr Butterfield was admitted, and due to the master's absence and the fact that he appeared to be having one fit after another, the matron sent him straight up to the hospital instead of keeping him in the receiving ward. Dr Hardwick was ordered by Superintendent Gillett to go to the workhouse and deal with the patient, but Dr Hardwick instructed his deputy, Dr Ready, to attend the man in his place. He did, but was told by the porter that there was no one in the receiving ward. This was at approximately 5.30 p.m. – so Dr Ready went away. The master, Mr Bates, realised what had happened on his return and called Dr Ready back to the workhouse hospital. He arrived at 6.30 p.m., and gave the unfortunate man some medication. He sat with him for about an hour before leaving. Unfortunately, however, Mr Butterfield died about 8.30 p.m. that same evening. Dr Hardwick defended himself by stating that Superintendent Gillett had no authority to summon him to the workhouse; he was very clear that under the Consolidated General Order a medical officer could only be summoned to the workhouse by the Guardians, the relieving officer or the master.

The inquest was held at the workhouse, and the coroner stated that a deputation of Mr Tomlinson (foreman of the jury) and Superintendent Gillett be sent to attend the next Guardians' meeting in order to remonstrate with them about Dr Hardwick's conduct in this matter. A week later, on the 6 June, the deputation from the inquest arrived to lay before the Guardians the facts connected with the death of Henry Butterfield. The Guardians were anxious to keep the press out of the meeting, but upon being told that it was a matter for public interest, they agreed. They argued that this would not be a precedent for the future, and the chair of the Guardians felt that Dr Hardwick had not acted inappropriately. The clerk stated that this was an isolated incident, and added there had been no complaints towards any of the medical officers or the master before (*RAMA*, 31 May 1863 and 6 June 1863).

The minutes record the enquiry, and reveal that the medical officer, the master and the nurse were all brought before the Guardians the following week. Their respective duties were read out to them from the Consolidated General Order. It was with great reluctance on the part of the Guardians, therefore, that they received Dr Hardwick's resignation in May 1891. The best thanks of the board 'was offered for services so long and faithfully rendered', for which he later received a pension of £40. His partner, Dr Alfred Robinson, was appointed as medical officer for the Rotherham workhouse in his place at the salary of £100 p.a.

The medical officers were responsible for the behaviour and discipline of the nurses in the workhouse hospital. These women, often paupers themselves, were usually untrained – and many had drink problems, as part of the salary was a daily supply of gin. Gin was comparatively cheap at that time, and many drank it in preference to the unhealthy water supply. In 1854, Mr Farnell, the Poor Law inspector, was called to the workhouse to enquire into the many complaints made against the hospital nurse regarding lack of extra supplies, solitary confinement and a diet of bread and water for any breaches of discipline. A special meeting was held on Thursday 1 June 1854 when he examined the statements of the nurse, the porter and some inmates (listed as Smith, Jarvis, Green and Robinson). Following this, the porter was asked to resign. The master handed in his notice, stating that he 'had got a better position', and an inmate called Elizabeth Robinson was given leave of absence for two days and one night. It was not until the end of this period of study that nursing was to become the professional occupation it is today. Although abuses by workhouse hospital nurses were commonly reported in the national and local press, on this occasion no reprimand was issued to the medical officer.

The medical officer for Kimberworth was Dr Bernard Walker. He first appears in the minutes in February 1866; not surprisingly, for the Guardians were demanding that he appear before the board 'to explain the reasons of so great a number of his patients requiring extra support'. Medical officers would get extra medical fees for attending a patient over long periods, and in September 1877 he applied to the Guardians for a fee of two guineas for attending Richard Lloyd daily. Mr Lloyd was suffering from an enlarged prostate and a paralysis of the bladder, and Dr Walker had been forced to use a catheter every day to ease his suffering. The extra costs were granted. Dr Walker was consulted in September 1887 when another outbreak of smallpox hit the town and he recommended that re-vaccination would be necessary in order to prevent the spread of the epidemic.

Nurses at vicarage, Moorgate Road.

From the minutes and in all his dealing with the Guardians, it would appear that Dr Walker was a very responsible and hard-working medical officer, so it is with some surprise that in June 1893, after more than thirty years as a medical officer, it is listed in the minutes that 'Mr Bernard Walker had been sent to 'The Quakers Retreat at York, an asylum'. The Local Government Board asked the Guardians to 'furnish a recent certificate showing whether he is likely to recover his sanity'. On receipt of the letter the clerk sent a copy of a letter from the superintendent of the asylum which had been received:

Sirs,

Mr Bernard Walker of Rotherham admitted to The Retreat at York is still of unsound mind and remains a patient in this institution. During the past two months Mr Walker has slightly improved and I consider that there is a reasonable hope of his ultimate recovery. I am still not able to give any decided opinion at present as to how long Mr Walker will remain of unsound mind. Under the most favourable circumstances it will be several months before he will be able to undertake any professional work. I would suggest that the Guardians would postpone for a further period of six months when I quite expect to be able to give more definite information.

Signed Bedford Pierce MD
Medical Superintendent to The Retreat, York

The following month matters had not improved for Dr Walker and it was agreed that, for the time being, they terminate their contract with him and enter into a fresh contract with some other qualified person. The Guardians agreed that if Dr Walker should recover they would avail themselves of his services once again. Unfortunately, however, Dr Walker did not recover and the state of his health became chronic in character. Dr Bedford Pierce wrote again in November 1893, 'I fear that the probability of ultimate recovery is very much reduced and even if he was discharged from the asylum it would be many months before he would be able to perform his duties'. His condition later deteriorated even further, and it was noted that the former medical officer was now 'under restraint'. The fact that a medical man could suffer from insanity does sadly emphasise that this condition could affect young and old, men and women, from any class in society; it was not a condition confined to the working classes.

The medical officer for Kimberworth who was appointed in Dr Bernard Walker's place was a Dr Lewis J. Weatherbe. The Local Government Board sanctioned the appointment in October 1893 after Dr Walker had been 'at The Retreat' for over twelve months. It was agreed that Dr Weatherbe's appointment would be made permanent. Dr Weatherbe worked very hard in his role as medical officer, but even he would have been unable to save some lives. In October 1896 a man was discovered on his hands and knees in the back yard of the Burns Hotel in Tinsley by the proprietor, Patrick Law. The man, a Robert Coy, aged forty-five, was described as 'a moulder', and was from Manchester. Coy had left the city to walk to Leeds looking for work. Patrick Law took him into the hotel and gave him tea, bread and butter and brandy. The man seemed to recover slightly and Patrick Law called PC Fretwell, who took Coy to the workhouse as it was obvious that he was suffering from hunger and fatigue. Coy told Fretwell that he had never been in a workhouse in his life and said that he would not go, but his condition was so bad that the policeman had no choice: Coy was admitted to the workhouse and sent to its hospital, where he was found to have a long-standing disease of the lung accelerated by exposure to cold and privation. He died a few days later, on the 9 October 1896. The coroner who held the inquest at the workhouse stated that he would have been better off in the workhouse where he would have had food and a roof over his head. The jury's verdict was that death had occurred from lung disease, privation and starvation (*RJ*, 17 October 1896). This case once again indicates the lengths to which people would go to find work rather than go into the workhouse.

In February 1900, the Boer War had been underway for four months when Dr Weatherbe valiantly informed the Guardians that he had joined the Gentleman's Corp of the Imperial Yeomanry and had been ordered for active service in the South African War. He asked permission to leave his deputy, Dr Coopland, in charge of his practice and he requested that the Guardians keep the position of medical officer for Kimberworth open for him during his absence. The Guardians agreed that a leave of absence be granted to him and the post would be kept open until his return. Thankfully, he did return to Rotherham in June 1901 to take up his position as medical officer once again, and the Guardians congratulated him 'on his safe and sound return after doing his noble duty on behalf of his sovereign and country'. No doubt Dr Weatherbe was amongst the celebrations which the soldiers took part in at Clifton Park.

THE SMALL-POX.

THE GUARDIANS AND THE CORPORATION.

IMPORTANT MEETING.

A fortnightly meeting of the Rotherham Board of Guardians was held on Monday morning at the workhouse, Mr J. Jubb (vice-chairman) presiding. The members present were:—Alderman Marsh, Messrs. W. Blunn (vice-chairman), Cox, Foers, Wells, Easton, Skinner, Jones, Parkin, Brightmore, Saxton, Wigfield, Whitworth, Walker, Booth, Hicks, Jackson, Harrop, and Wood......The CLERK read a letter from Dr. Walker, vaccination officer, as follows:—"I regret to have to inform you that small-pox of a virulent type has broken out in my vaccination district, having been imported here from Sheffield, and I am desirous that you will kindly obtain permission from the Rotherham Board of Guardians for my being allowed to vaccinate and re-vaccinate whenever called upon to do so, without my being restricted to time or place. The law provides for such an exceptional period, and the urgency of such a course being immediately adopted is fully manifested by the cases I have on hand, the efficiently vaccinated suffering but temporary inconvenience, the non-vaccinated—or imperfectly done—are in imminent danger, and will, if they recover, be disfigured for life. If my application is granted, I would be prepared to revaccinate all persons over 12 years of age at the vaccination station, Howard street, Rotherham, every Thursday at 2.30 p.m., and at my own surgery every morning (Sunday excepted) at 9.30, and should be pleased to have notice to that effect given to the public.—Believe me, yours faithfully, BERNARD WALKER, P.S.—It would give me great pleasure to take any gentleman to view some of these cases, who is at all dubious about the efficacy

In September 1892 the Guardians were so satisfied with the conduct of the medical officers they gave them all an increase in salary. The Local Government Board immediately wrote to find out the reason for this pay increase. The Guardians informed them:

> For several years past the Guardians have had under their consideration applications for increases in salary but they deemed it desirable to get out statements showing the area population etc relating to each medical officer's district and that after full consideration of all the facts the board came to the conclusion that the salary should be increased and that the grounds were in every case in consequence of the greatly increased population and also the labour now devolving upon them. The board are of the opinion that the officers are fully entitled to the increases given and consider that they will not then be overpaid.

As stated, the medical officers did not live in at the workhouse and, providing they lived reasonably near, they could continue to fulfil their duties and combine them with their own private patients. The only other workhouse officer able to do this was the workhouse chaplain.

Opposite: Part of Dr Walker's recommends re-vaccination to prevent the spread of smallpox (*RAMA*, 10 September 1887).

four

The Workhouse Chaplain

Initially the post of the workhouse chaplain was advertised in the local press and the candidate was duly elected by the Guardians from the applications received. By February of 1850, however, the post became synonymous with the vicar of Rotherham's position at All Saints' parish church in the centre of the town. The post of workhouse chaplain was seen as a prestigious role which would compliment his other parish duties, and like the role of the medical officer it was not very well paid. Yet it seems that the role of chaplain to the Rotherham workhouse attracted a group of very caring and dedicated churchmen who did much to make the lives of the paupers of Rotherham as pleasant as they could be, given their position.

The roles and responsibilities of the Rotherham workhouse chaplain were outlined in the minutes for July 1841 where it was agreed by the Guardians that he would read the service and preach a sermon in the workhouse every Sunday 'in the forenoon' and that he administer the sacraments at Christmas, Easter and Whitsuntide. The religious services for the inmates and workhouse officers took place in the dining hall and were accompanied by the harmonium, the children of the workhouse making up the choir. It was felt by the Guardians that all services for the inmates were to be held inside the building itself in order for discipline to be maintained. The proximity in Rotherham of the many beerhouses and pubs might prove too much of a temptation for the inmates.

Once again the list of workhouse chaplains is extensive, but it is worth mentioning that Revd Richard Moseley was appointed (the first chaplain to take on the dual role of vicar of All Saints' Parish church as well as that of the workhouse chaplain). His appointment, as with other subsequent chaplains, had to be sanctioned by the Archbishop of York. According to the local newspapers, the Revd Moseley was a well-loved character, and he dutifully looked after the religious duties for his parish and the Rotherham workhouse for thirty years (from 1842 to October 1872, when ill health forced him to resign). He was described by George Gummer in his *Reminiscences* as being:

> ...short in figure with snow white whiskers and trailing one leg owing to some infirmity. He was frequently seen on his way from the Vicarage to the Church, or on a visit to the poor, to whom he gave nearly the whole of his stipend of £300 per annum. Endeared by

All Saints' parish church.

his parishioners, worshipped by the poor it was a great loss to the town when advancing years and declining health caused him to resign.

(This appears on www.rotherhamweb.co.uk.) Revd Moseley was able to inform the Guardians of the name of his successor as the Reverend William Newton. He also hinted that 'the gentlemen had means', an expression used in those days to indicate that he had a substantial private income which would compensate for the fact that the salary of the vicar of the parish church at Rotherham was not a substantial one.

The letter from Revd William Newton, the new vicar of Rotherham, offering his services as workhouse chaplain was received by the Guardians in November 1872 and he was appointed at the salary of £40 p.a. The new chaplain was a great believer in the Temperance Movement and was unhappy in the squalid conditions of the town's housing. It was felt that the working man would often prefer to seek refuge in the local hostelries rather than the unsanitary conditions of his own home.

Above Revd Richard Moseley.

Right Revd William Newton.

Following a temperance mission held in Rotherham in 1876 with the Archbishop of York, the chaplain opened a cocoa and coffee house at the bottom of Wellgate in 1877 which remained open for two years. It was extremely popular with the working classes and as a result was soon found to be too small. Revd Newton then began his greatest achievement in the building of St Georges Hall at the corner of Howard Street and Effingham Street at a cost of £6,000; it opened in October 1878. The Temperance Movement became popular in Rotherham mainly due to the efforts of the successive workhouse chaplains and many Bible classes arranged outings. It was thought that arranged outings such as these would be an alternative to spending time in the public houses of the town.

It was therefore a very sad moment for the inmates of the workhouse and for the town when the Revd William Newton's sudden death was announced in February 1879. He had been the chaplain for only seven years and during that time it was stated that 'no one has ever done as much for the town'. Revd Newton had been staying at the house of Mr Goodwin of Newton Barrells Park, near Birmingham, on 18 February and on the previous evening had fallen whilst skating, after colliding with his brother, Revd Horace Newton. There had been some delay in getting him off the ice, resulting in a chill and causing his lungs to become congested. Nevertheless, he had appeared well and it was reported that evening that he bade his wife 'goodnight and God bless you'. At 6 a.m. the following morning she found him dead. The people of Rotherham had expected his return in a few days, and the first intimation that this would not happen was the tolling of the bells from Rotherham parish church. His death was a great shock to many people and particularly the inmates of the workhouse

Slums at Lower Millgate.

The poor condition of children in Westgate (note the barefoot child).

Coffee and Cocoa House, Wellgate, 1885.

and the poor of the town. It was agreed that until a new chaplain could be elected that the churchwardens would continue the work of chaplain to the workhouse (*RAMA*, 22 February 1879).

The next workhouse chaplain of note was appointed in January 1882; the Right Revd Dr Henry Cheetham applied for the position of chaplain and was unanimously elected. During his chaplaincy it was agreed with the Guardians that a Band of Hope for the workhouse children would be held at the workhouse and it was agreed that children aged between seven and fourteen years would be allowed to attend. The children would be encouraged to take abstinence pledges and they would attend lectures on the 'evils of drink'. Activities such as tea parties and outings were planned where hymns would be sung and games played providing a welcome break from the workhouse routines.

However, for reasons which are unclear, the following month the chaplain resigned and the Revd John Quirke was appointed in his place. He continued to involve the workhouse children in the Band of Hope activities and the minutes record that in August 1884 the children were invited to join in the procession and gala to be held on the 25th at Conisbrough. Revd John Quirke also invited the workhouse children on an outing to Cleethorpes on Friday 23 July 1884. This would have been a great treat for the poor children, many of whom would not have visited the seaside before. He asked that two officers accompany the children and this was left to be arranged by the master. Revd Quirk did not forget his other duties and as the vicar of All

Greasbrough Bible Class outing, 1880.

Souls he also led the special thanksgiving service on Sunday 19 June 1887 for Queen Victoria's Golden Jubilee. Revd Quirk kept the post as chaplain to the workhouse until December 1889 when he resigned to take up a new post in Wetherby. He wrote a letter to his parishioners which was printed in the local newspaper: 'that to change at all is always a trial: but when happiness in work and the kindness of ever kind and helpful friends have caused the roots to strike deep then the removal is more difficult to accomplish and hard to face'. (*RAMA*, 26 October 1889.) There is no doubt that he had been a most popular workhouse chaplain, and I would imagine that he was greatly missed by the workhouse inmates.

Revd W.B. Pym was elected into the post of workhouse chaplain in March 1893 at the same salary for the last fifty years of £40 per year. The poor housing condition in Rotherham had not escaped the new chaplain's notice, and in November 1897 the Revd Pym condemned the housing of the poor which he christened 'slumdums' from the pulpit of the parish church. He stated that 'in this matter our town is in reproach'. He castigated the town councillors who were attending the service to take this matter up as soon as possible. As the *Rotherham and Masbrough Advertiser* revealed on the 20 November 1897, he continued:

> I have visited courts during the last week in which I defy any human being to live either a happy or a clean life and there are many such. If you disagree go and look for yourselves. The slums are out of sight but it is the duty of public men to sweep these slums away.

Parish church choir outing, 1908.

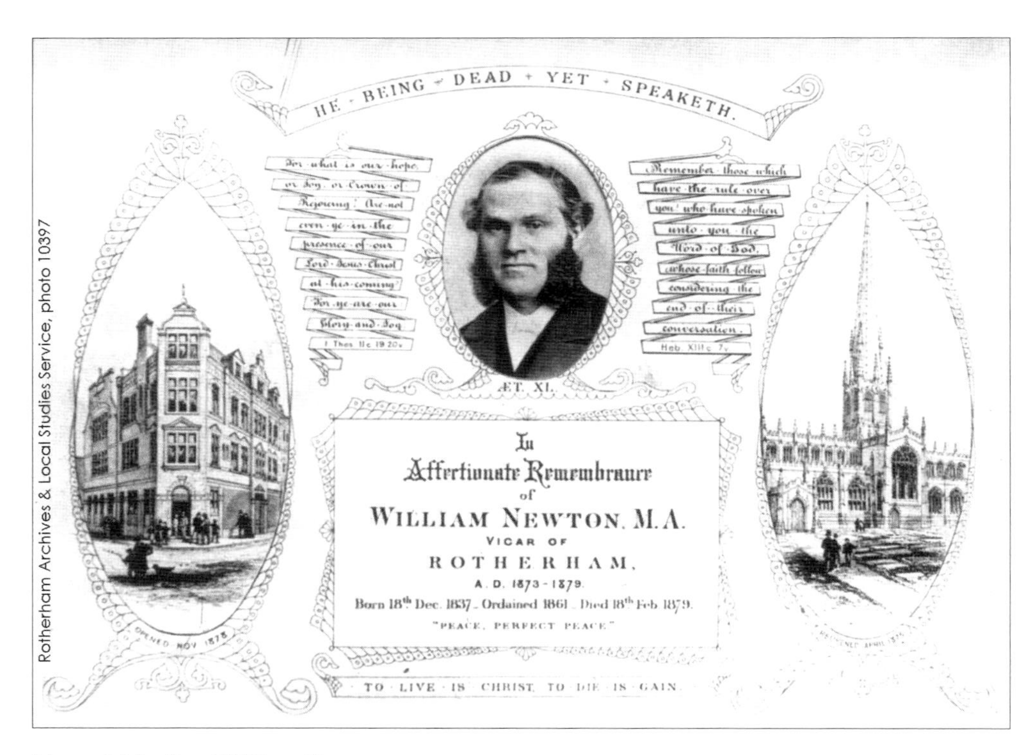

Memorial for Revd William Newton.

Unfortunately it was not until 1933 that many of these slums were finally eliminated from the town. It has to be said that in Rotherham, as in other industrial towns, the condition of the housing of the poor people of the town was not a high priority. It was noted in the minutes of December 1853 that the attention of the Guardians should 'be called to the unsuitable accommodation in the many dwellings of the labouring classes'. It was noted that 'such unhealthy dwellings are reported frequently as unfit for human habitation and in the case of sickness, the cost to the poor rate is very severe'. The impact of industrialisation on the town of Rotherham had increased its population and as a consequence, the state of the houses deteriorated. A particular source of disease was experienced in the vicinity of the old Shambles in the Market Place. These were cattle markets where beasts were killed and blood, faeces and other matter flowed into the streets and alleyways.

By August 1898 the Revd Pym had accepted the prestigious post of the Bishopric of Mauritius and was consecrated in St Paul's Cathedral on 29 September 1898 when he left Rotherham and the workhouse inmates (*RAMA*, 20 August 1898). There was a delay in the appointment of the next chaplain and it was not until July 1899 that the Revd John William Goodall was finally elected as the new workhouse chaplain and was very much welcomed to the Guardians. He was known to the previous incumbent and was delighted on the morning of his investiture when he received a letter from the Bishop of Mauritius expressing his delight that 'his successor to Rotherham was a dear

Revd Henry Cheetham, 1881.

Above St Peter's Mission to Boston Park, 1895.

Left Revd John Quirke, seen here in a group of vicars and curates, in 1883.

Above Parish church outing to Cleethorpes, 1908.

Right Revd Walter R. Pym and curates outside the parish church.

Above Some of the 'slumdums', as described by Revd W.R. Pym.

Left The Shambles, 1880–95.

Rotherham Archives & Local Studies Service, photo 10833

Revd John William Goodall.

and valued friend' (*RAMA*, 17 June 1899). He applied to the Guardians offering his services as the workhouse chaplain the same month and was gratefully accepted. No further mention is made in the minutes regarding Revd Goodall, but he remained the vicar of Rotherham parish church up to the end of the period of study.

It seems as time went by that the plight of the paupers were viewed with more sympathy and a deeper understanding about the terrible conditions which forced them into the workhouse. As the minutes indicate, many small gifts and kindnesses were shown to the paupers as time went on and they had regular treats and outings. The press reflected this opinion and reported the many kindnesses of the patrons towards the workhouse inmates. Descriptions of outings and particularly the Christmas Day celebrations were published in the local newspapers, and included in many of these celebrations were the workhouse chaplains. It is my feeling that due to the kindness and hard work of these chaplains, the inmates of the Rotherham workhouse seemed to be viewed with more dignity than in the early years of the workhouse system.

five

The Master and Matron

The role of the master and matron of any workhouse was a role which carried a lot of authority. In some workhouses the master took absolute charge of who was admitted to the workhouse – and this would include the Guardians themselves. It was also widely reported that matrons used some inmates as their own personal servants, and misuse of power was noted in many cases. Other officers of the workhouse – such as the schoolteachers, the porter and his wife and the nurses – had to ask permission of the master if they wished to leave the workhouse for any reason, and the minutes hold many complaints when this procedure was not always followed. In such a position of power it would be inevitable that this would lead to disagreements and complaints, and Rotherham workhouse was no exception.

It seems the master's duties were numerous and included admitting paupers to the workhouse, maintaining order and discipline, registering all births and deaths in the workhouse, inspecting the building and reporting to the Guardians every board day. He was to say prayers morning and evening with the inmates and say grace before each meal. His wife was expected to be his deputy and to supervise the female wards and undertake all the domestic arrangements for the workhouse. She was responsible for searching any of the female inmates and ensuring that the women and children's clothes were changed every week. The master and matron were jointly responsible to the Guardians for the smooth running routine and the security of the house. They were also responsible for the tight schedule which was expected to be adhered to as closely as possible. With such power it is not surprising that abuses would be recorded.

One report which was substantiated involved the master of Hoo workhouse, James Miles, who was accused in 1840 of flogging inmates, women and children alike. A surprise visit by the Poor Law inspector in April 1901 revealed the absence of the master and matron at Martley workhouse in Worcestershire. When the inspector spoke to the inmates he was surprised at the liberal discipline which he found. Inmates were allowed to go to the public house; indeed, one boasted that he had just returned with 6d worth of gin. They alleged that Mr and Mrs Battersea, the master and his wife, had frequently been found in a state of intemperance. It was also alleged that the pauper's food was poor, the Christmas treat had been withdrawn and it was noted that the children were ill clothed and dirty (Martley Workhouse, www.archive.worcesternews.co.uk/2001/4/6/331276.html). It seems that the regime in many workhouses was determined by the master and matron.

The salary of the master and matron was, like the other officers in the workhouse, to include board, lodging, laundry and beer allowance. There was no qualification asked for the post and only the most elementary education was needed to complete the administrative tasks required. It was inevitable that the educated schoolteachers would see themselves as at least on a par with the status of master and matron, although it seems their position was much lower. Nevertheless, throughout the early minutes there are constant complaints and accusations from other officers (such as the porter and his wife and the schoolmaster or schoolmistress) who would be expected to deputise for the master.

The position of porter was quite an important one, and like the master and matron often led to a misuse of power. Peter Higginbotham's website, www.workhouses.org.uk, tells of how, in 1840, a local newspaper reported that the porter of the Kidderminster workhouse was taken before the magistrate accused of ill treating a pauper child of eight years called Perks. It seems that Perks had wet himself, 'which caused great offence' to the porter; as punishment, he placed the boy in a sack hanging from a beam. The master, hearing groans, cut the bag down and found the boy doubled up in the bag where he had been suspended all morning. It seems it was not the first time this treatment had been meted out by the porter. The tension of working in such close proximity every day of the week naturally took its toll and the many clashes between the officers of the Rotherham workhouse were reported in the minutes. A sense of frustration is recorded in August 1849 when a circular letter is received from the Poor Law Board following, once again, an investigation of complaints between the workhouse officers. In it, the Poor Law inspector urges the officers of the Rotherham workhouse that, 'there must be an absence of personal feeling and that helping each other in their duties is a part of their duty'.

Mr and Mrs Worsley were appointed as the first Rotherham union workhouse master and matron and their duties were to commence on the 22 February 1838. For the next ten years they served the Guardians faithfully before committing what was considered a grievous fault. In August 1848, it was reported by the visiting committee that the master was responsible for breaches in the separation of the sexes in the workhouse. It seems that certain men had on several occasions 'improperly had access to the women's yard during the day and their lodging rooms at night'. The separation of the sexes was a crucial element of workhouse life and the Guardians would have been very displeased at this lack of attention. It was reported that such 'dereliction of duty' gave male and female paupers 'an opportunity of making assignations and of having communication with each other'. Before he could be sacked, however, it seems that the master died – and it was common practice that if either master or matron passed away, the other partner would have to leave. Mrs Worsley tendered her own resignation on 9 October 1848.

The next appointed master and matron was Mr and Mrs Boyes from Ecclesfield workhouse in Sheffield. To ensure better conduct, Mr and Mrs Boyes were asked to

SAVAGE ATTACK UPON THE MATRON OF THE ROTHERHAM WORKHOUSE BY A PAUPER LUNATIC. — On Thursday morning. Mrs. Turner, the matron of the Rotherham Workhouse, was the victim of a savage assault by a pauper lunatic of the Workhouse, who was afterwards pronounced by the medical officer to be insane. About a quarter to eleven o'clock, Mrs. Turner went into the Day room of the Workhouse, and saw that Joseph Gill, twenty-three years of age, was not going about his work of cleaning the chamber. She requested him to move a form, whereupon, without saying a word, he ran towards her, and savagely kicked her on the lower part of the body. The ruffian, who has been an inmate of the Workhouse for about four months, and who had previously been quiet in his behaviour, was removed by force to the lunatic ward. On his way thither he bit the porter's hand very severely, and also violently kicked him ; and on the room being reached a straight jacket had to be placed upon him. Mrs. Turner became so ill in consequence of the assault, that she had to retire to her bed, and during the whole of yesterday was confined to her room, the medical officer, Dr. Hardwicke, stating that she was very badly injured. He certified Gill to be a lunatic, and advised his removal to an asylum. The removal will be effected as speedily as possible.

Report of Mrs Turner being kicked by a pauper lunatic.

give a surety of £100. They began their employment at the Rotherham workhouse in November 1848; less than nine months later a complaint was laid before the Guardians from the master regarding the conduct of the schoolmaster and schoolmistress 'leaving the house unknown to him'. A counter complaint was heard by the Guardians from the schoolmaster, Mr Samuel Ellis, in December of the same year against the master. Things quietened down for a short while but then a further allegation about Mrs Boyes was heard in March 1851: the porter and his wife alleged that she was a 'woman of intemperate habits' who had 'acted unruly in front of the inmates'. There is predictably no record of the investigation, but the master handed in both his and his wife's notice the following month, which was accepted by the Guardians. Perhaps his part was viewed with leniency and the Guardians were more concerned about his wife's behaviour, as he later applied for a testimonial and received a glowing one from the Guardians for another position.

By 1860 the master is listed as Mr George Bates and his wife. Due to missing minutes it is unclear when he was appointed, but already the Guardians were in the middle of investigating a serious complaint to the Poor Law inspector about a breach of security caused by him. The only clue we have is an entry into the minutes for that week recording that 'once again the security of the workhouse had been lax'. The Guardians informed the master and matron in no uncertain terms that 'they were responsible for the security of the whole house by day and night'. Matters seemed to have quietened down until the master and matron were summoned before the board to give an explanation in July 1866, when it was noted in the visitor's book that 'an improper consequence had taken place between a male and a female pauper each of the parties being weak minded'.

The couple appeared before the Guardians the following week at the workhouse 'to give such explanation as may be necessary of the circumstances under which the paupers were permitted to associate together'. There are no further entries on this subject and unfortunately a few months later, in September 1866, Mr Bates informed the Guardians about the death of his wife. As in previous cases, he had to tender his resignation, and a Mr and Mrs Mitchell were elected the same month.

They were quite a young couple for the position (Mr Mitchell was aged thirty-three and his wife was twenty-seven) and both had worked at the Sheffield workhouse school. The young age of the master and his wife caused some consternation therefore on 1 July 1867 when Mrs Mitchell gave birth to a child. The role of master and matron had previously been advertised as 'not to have any encumbrances'. It may be that the Guardians had been unaware of the pregnancy as when the master informed the Guardians about the birth of the child, they resolved to consider it the following week. On this occasion they were unable to make a decision and the question was passed to the Poor Law inspector for his consideration. There is no further mention in the minutes of the matter and the couple continued in their role, so it looks like the problem was resolved.

However, it seems the peace of the workhouse officials was broken once more in August 1868 when complaints were once again received by the Guardians from both the master and the porter. It was noted in the minutes that copies of their statements were taken and sent to the Poor Law inspector to examine, and a special meeting was convened on Thursday 3 September 1868 to examine the charges. Once again there is no evidence of what the charges were, but the conclusion reached by the Guardians was that, 'There have been great remissions on the part of the master in the management of the house and that he be cautioned as to his conduct for the future.'

It could be that the master was drunk, as previously it had been noted in the minutes that Mr Mitchell 'was said to be drunk': whatever the reason, it led to the master and matron's resignation in September 1870. When being appointed to the post of master, Mr Mitchell also had to give names as sureties for the way in which he carried out his duties and as part of his bond he had given the name of Mr Charles Henry Turner, the station master at Rotherham railway station. In October 1870 Mr Turner applied for, and became, master of Rotherham workhouse.

The role of master and matron, it seems, involved a degree of violence, and only two years later it was reported that Mrs Turner had been savagely kicked by a pauper lunatic at the workhouse. Mrs Turner had instructed Joseph Gill, aged twenty-three, to clean his chamber. Instead, he ran at her and kicked her on 'the lower part of the body'. She was so ill that she was forced to take to her bed and the pauper was forcibly restrained in a strait jacket.

Sadly, four years later, on 13 April 1878, the master announced the death of his wife, Mrs Margaritte Turner, who was aged just thirty-seven. Perhaps as an indication of the Guardians' complete faith in Mr Turner – and as a complete reversal to previous protocol – it was agreed that a single matron be advertised for in the local newspapers. There were forty applications for the post, which the assessment committee whittled down to the four applications submitted to the Guardians. Margaritta Gilpin, aged twenty-six, an assistant matron at West Bromwich, was appointed. Soon afterwards, and not for the first time, Cupid arrived on the scene: it was reported in the local paper of April of the following year that the marriage of Mr Turner (aged fifty-seven) and Miss Gilpin had taken place. (*RAMA*, 10 April 1879.) Despite the ban on 'encumbrances', the 1881 census returns list a five-month-old son named Bernard Henry. But only four years later, in February 1885, condolences were sent to Mrs Turner on the death of her husband following an illness.

The post of master and matron was advertised once again in February – stating very clearly this time that the couple had to 'have no encumbrances'. The advert offered a salary of £90 p.a. plus the usual rations, board, washing and meals. The Guardians further requested that the couple not be 'under 40 years of age', suggesting no more babies were to be born to the master and matron! Mr and Mrs Walton of Romford Street, Manchester, were appointed in March 1885 at the salary of £60 and £30 respectively. Once again, however, misfortune dogged the heels of the master and matron and less than five years later, in January 1890, Mr Walton informed the board of the death of his wife. He requested and it was agreed that his niece, Miss Lucy Lawton, be appointed as a temporary substitute, an appointment which was later made permanent.

This was quite a diversion from the normal way of doing things. It was not a fortunate decision, for just a few months later, in November 1890, both Mr Walton and Miss Lawton were forced to resign from their posts. It seems that Mr Walton had allowed his niece to stay in the workhouse before she was appointed as matron, where it was alleged that 'she was treated as an officer of the workhouse'. She was also accused of not supervising the inmates sufficiently when she was matron, resulting in one of the paupers becoming pregnant. The reasons were sent to the Local Government Board following an investigation which proved that Mr Walton had 'seriously neglected his duties'. The Guardians demanded that Mr Walton hand in his resignation without delay.

ANOTHER day in the workhouse is portrayed by one of the Memory Lane photographs this week.

Sent in by Mrs Irene Crowson, of Old Whittington, Chesterfield, it shows her father-in-law, John Henry William Crowson, as a child with his parents and staff at Rotherham Workhouse in the 1890s.

His father, John Thomas Crowson, was the master of the workhouse and the matron is pictured on the right.

Mr and Mrs Crowson (Courtesy of Mrs Irene Crowson).

The minutes report that the board also considered that the evidence shows that Miss Lawton had neither the training nor experience requisite for the office of matron in such a workhouse as Rotherham, and they required her also to resign her office. The posts of master and matron were once again advertised.

In July 1897 Mr and Mrs Crowson from Louth was appointed at a salary of £150 p.a. There is an (undated) picture from the *Rotherham Advertiser* of the master and matron, Mr and Mrs Crowson, with their staff behind them. They are sitting in the middle of the picture and both sit with a quiet air of authority. Mr Crowson's hands are folded across his chest and he looks the picture of Victorian respectability. His wife is seated at the side of him with her elaborate bonnet and exquisite embroidery at the front of her dress. A child – identified by Mrs Irene Crowson as her father-in-law, John Henry William Crowson [Harry], born in 1897 – stands in front of the picture. The child's dress is elaborate even for the clothes of the period: he wears a suit which would not look out of place in *Little Lord Fauntleroy*. He is wearing an elaborate lace collar and a hat at a jaunty angle on his head with a huge feather in it. He looks the picture of a pampered and much-loved child.

As we have seen, the role of master and matron held a lot of power and it is therefore not surprising that such power was abused. Many cases of cruelty were reported from the positions of master and matron and Rotherham is not exceptional in this matter. The master of the Andover Union workhouse, Mr Colin McDougal (a former Sergeant Major), and his wife ruled the workhouse with a rod of iron. Mrs McDougal was reputed to be 'a violent lady'. They ran the workhouse like a penal colony, keeping expenditure and food rations to a minimum, much to the approval of the Andover Guardians. The inmates were forced to eat with their fingers and any man who tried to speak to his wife during mealtimes would serve a spell in the refractory cell (www.victorianweb.org/history/poorlaw/andover.html). Many of these abuses were not observed by the Guardians at Andover as they were not used to visiting the workhouse and had no idea about the regime under which the paupers suffered. The Guardians at Rotherham were more careful about the way in which their officers behaved and they dealt with any complaint quite seriously. Many of those complaints, as we shall see, came from the teachers at the workhouse.

six

Teachers and Education in the Workhouse

Sometimes it must have felt that the teachers were as much inmates of the workhouse as the children. They were expected to be at the beck and call of the master and the care of the children was their responsibility in and out of school hours. The schoolmaster and schoolmistresses main role was to teach the children, escort them for any visits out of the house and be responsible for discipline and the children's appearance. The very young ages of some of the teachers leads one to believe that this was probably a first post; which was possibly entered into to gain experience before going on to more a responsible position. The first workhouse schoolteachers were untrained and no qualifications were required. Consequentially, amongst the other officers they were not seen as figures of authority; only the children regarded them in this light. Qualification for the teachers improved after 1848 when the treasury began direct grants to Guardians to subsidise workhouse teachers' pay, which was now related to their qualifications.

In Rotherham workhouse it was noted that not much attention was paid to the children's environment and this was reported in the local newspaper by a reporter who had looked at the school. The schoolroom was described in April 1872 in the *Rotherham and Masbrough Advertiser* as:

> …perhaps the least inspiring part of the workhouse and appears to have been selected with a grim notion that in all but prison-like gloom the mind would be rapidly developed. It is certainly hoped so for the sake of the amiable schoolmistress Miss Geraghty as well as the children that the lessons are not long for they ought under the circumstances to have a superabundance of intellectual brilliance to overcome the shadows of the veritable blackboards and inevitable low forms. As there are several unoccupied rooms, may we suggest that it would be possible for the Guardians to appropriate a part of the establishment to the educational requirements of the union where there is an abundance of light and an occasional gleam of sunshine.

ROTHERHAM UNION.

APPOINTMENT OF SCHOOLMISTRESS.

NOTICE IS HEREBY GIVEN, THAT THE Board of Guardians of the above named Union, will, at their Weekly Meeting, to be held on Monday, the 21st instant, proceed to elect a properly qualified person to fill the office of SCHOOLMISTRESS at the Union Workhouse.

The salary will be £16 per annum, with such further sum as the Committee of Council on Education may award in their certificate, together with Board, Washing, and Lodging in the Workhouse; and an allowance of 1s. per week in lieu of beer.

Preference will be given to candidates holding Certificates of the Committee of Council on Education.

Candidates are requested to send applications in their own hand-writing, stating age, residence, past and present occupation, with testimonials of character, temper and competency, to the Clerk of the Union, on or before the 19th instant.

Canvassing the Guardians is prohibited.

By order of the Board,
JNO. BARRAS,
Clerk to the Guardians.

Advertisement answered by Louise Mason (*RJ*, 3 October 1857).

Being taught in such an environment must have been felt by the workhouse children and added to their low feelings of self worth. The futility of educating workhouse children was discussed in the national press (which was reflected in society's idea that educating workhouse children was pointless as they would soon return to a profligate life on leaving the workhouse). Nevertheless, the Guardians and the Poor Law Board felt that giving workhouse children a minimum standard of basic education would instil in them the values of hard work and keep them out of the workhouses of the future.

As always, the Guardians' aim was to reduce costs, and initially only a schoolmistress was advertised for and elected. Miss Ann Thickett, aged twenty-three, became the first schoolmistress for the Rotherham workhouse soon after it opened. She was appointed in September 1839 at a salary of £10 p.a. with 'the same provision of rations as the master and matron'. Schoolmistresses from here on are recorded in the minutes (and they come and go with regularity), but suffice it to say that it was not until 1847 that a schoolmaster, Mr Samuel Ellis, was employed at a salary of £30 p.a.

A further schoolmaster was appointed following Mr Ellis's resignation in January 1850; Mr Henry Carilon was elected at the same salary.

As earlier noted, discipline was the responsibility of the teachers, and they were allowed to use corporal punishment to correct their young charges. Flogging of young children was an accepted form of punishment inflicted by schoolteachers or by the master himself. It is to be hoped that Rotherham workhouse school exercised more restraint than Lambeth workhouse. The *Times* of 23 January 1838 reported that a 'young boy' called Henry Bailey who came from the Lambeth workhouse was sent to the Norwood House of Industry, where they discovered that his back, thighs, arms and legs were covered in black marks. When asked who had hit him, he replied that Mr Rowe, the schoolmaster, and a nurse belonging to the Lambeth workhouse had beaten him for taking a drop of beer. The boy died six days later and the post-mortem showed the boy was much reduced and wasted with a disease of the lungs. Marks such as the buckle end of a belt were found. Perhaps fortunately for the schoolmaster, Mr Rowe, he died on the day the boy was admitted to Norwood. The jury returned a verdict of death caused by a disease of the lungs.

The minutes record that Mr George Paul was appointed schoolmaster at Rotherham workhouse in July 1857 and Louise Mason was appointed schoolmistress in October of the same year. At this time the workhouse school was regularly visited and the pupils inspected by the Poor Law inspector and the Guardians, and it seems there were some improvements. The local newspaper, the *Rotherham Journal*, had reported on 13 February 1858 that:

> Workhouse school Guardians attended at the workhouse for the purpose of inspecting the school. After a thorough examination of the children which occupied upwards of two hours, Reverend J. Reece proceeded in a very able and feeling manner to address the children and distribute prizes of books to them. The result of the examination was highly satisfactory and reflected great credit on the schoolmaster and schoolmistress, Mr Paul and Miss Mason.

By this time there were thirty-eight children in the workhouse school. Both teachers had only been in post for seven months, so it was of great credit to them. It would seem that Mr Paul and Miss Mason hit it off famously, as three years later in May 1860 the schoolmaster wrote a letter to the Rotherham Guardians to inform them that he and the schoolmistress had got married. He asked for the Guardians' approval; instead, the Guardians were outraged. They reported that, 'this board think that Mr Paul should have communicated his intention to marry with Miss Mason before it was solemnised and as a consequence have disqualified themselves for their present situations in Rotherham union workhouse'.

There is no reason given in the minutes for the Guardians' disapproval. As a result, the newly-wed Mr and Mrs Paul gave notice of their resignation the following month. Mr Paul later applied to the Guardians for a testimonial, which was given (stating that 'he was well able to fulfil the duties of a schoolmaster in any area where married persons are eligible for such appointment.').

One appointment for a workhouse teacher was a disaster. In June 1861 the schoolmaster was John Croft, aged twenty-eight. His address was 19 Spring Gardens, Doncaster. A few weeks later the Guardians received a report from Pocklington School, where Mr Croft had been employed as a schoolmaster in his previous post, 'as to the manner in which he had performed his duties'. The reply is not recorded, but the Rotherham Guardians informed the Poor Law Board that 'this board is not satisfied' and a letter written by the chair, Hon. Revd Mr Howard, was sent to this effect. The reason for the Guardians' annoyance was reports about his negligence of the workhouse children from both the school inspector and the visiting committee which were put to the Poor Law Board in November 1861. It looked like the Guardians had made an unfortunate appointment and would have liked to get rid of Mr Crofts. After serving a six-month probationary period it was common for the Poor Law Board to sanction the post, but in this instance they insisted on another six months of probation. Nevertheless, by February there were still complaints and the Guardians reported sadly, 'That the Poor Law Board again be informed that the visitors report the boys in the workhouse school are much neglected and that the schoolmaster has been reproved for such neglect previously, they have no expectation that he will improve.'

In April 1862 Mr Croft was given leave of absence for two weeks and following a letter sent to him from the Poor Law Board he was given further leave in June for a week. Were the Guardians giving him the opportunity to find another place? It seems to have worked, as his resignation was received in August 1862. You can almost hear the sighs of relief from the Guardians when he resigns. Their testimonial for him appears to be very tongue in cheek: it states that Mr Croft, 'was elected schoolmaster of this union from a number of candidates solely from the quality of his testimonials which were unexceptional. He has been here fifteen months. His ability as a teacher is best proved by the report of Her Majesties Inspector of Schools to which we beg to refer.' As the reports were not very good, it was not the kind of reference one would wish to receive.

The Rotherham Guardians seem to be having no more luck with other schoolmasters. On 25 August 1862, Mr George Jeff was appointed. Like the previous schoolmaster, he was admonished for the neglected state of the workhouse children. Having been in post only three months, he was asked to appear before the board to explain why the visiting committee had complained about the dirty appearance of the boys. Strangely enough, in April 1866, both schoolteachers, Mr George Jeff and Miss Biggins, handed in their resignation on the same day. Was this romance at work once again? We will never know. Certainly they would be in no doubt of the Guardians' reactions should they wish to marry.

Unfortunately, there were no applications for the post in May 1866 as a result of the advertisements in the local newspapers and Mr Jeff was instructed to make the best arrangements he could until the advertisements for both schoolmaster and schoolmistress could be inserted once more. Although the adverts were for both posts, no other schoolmaster was appointed. Was this because the post was not seen as a popular one, or could the Rotherham Guardians have become more wary of teachers marrying their counterparts?

Once again, a period of very high staff turnover occurred, with countless new teachers who did not stay in post for very long, again suggesting a tension between the officers of the workhouse. Perhaps as a result of this, in October 1881 it was moved by Revd William Blazeby (and seconded by Mr Whitworth) that the children of the workhouse be sent to schools outside the workhouse, a suggestion which was approved. The children were sent to the Wellgate Board School. The scheme was very successful and was approved of by Mr J.S. Davy, the Government Inspector of Schools. As reported in the *Rotherham and Masbrough Advertiser* of 10 March 1884, he sent a letter to the Doncaster Guardians, who were considering reinstating the workhouse school. He told them:

> Nothing has been done in my time so beneficial to the workhouse children as sending them out to school in the town. The children are generally healthier and more intelligent and most important of all, they are happier. The break in the monotony of daily life within the workhouse walls was everything to them.

Attending the board school in the town would ensure that the children had a release from the workhouse for short periods. The teachers would have been aware that the children came from the workhouse, but by this time they were treated more sympathetically. It is to be hoped that even the rudimentary education they received would have been of use to the children; sadly, with the intervention of two World Wars, the probability was that workhouse education only prepared them to be cannon fodder for the wars which were to follow. Meanwhile, the prospect for the schoolteachers would not be much better than the workhouse children. Men may have gone on to teach in other schools or become tutors for middle-class children, but the prospects for female teachers would not be improved for many years to come.

seven

Giving Birth and Children in the Workhouse

In the Guardians' minutes there is very little information about the women who gave birth in the workhouse – but what can be surmised is that they can not have expected any compassion, comfort or even hygienic conditions in which to bring a new child into the world. Giving birth in the lying-in ward of any workhouse must have been grim to say the least. The midwives were possibly older, infirm women. The Poor Law reformer Louisa Twining vividly portrays what it was like to give birth in a workhouse in London:

> The lying in ward… which was only a general ward without even screens, had an old inmate in it who we discovered to have an ulcerated leg and cancer of the breast: yet she did nearly everything for the women and the babies, and often delivered them too. The women's hair was not combed, it was 'not lucky' to do so and washing was at a discount. The doctor and myself could not imagine at first why the temperature went up, and the babies nearly always got bad eyes and did badly. (Geoffrey Rivett, Poor Law Infirmaries, http://nhshistory.net/poor_law_infirmaries.htm)

The conditions at the Rotherham lying-in wards could hardly have been any better than these. But the largest area for criticism was not the conditions of the ward but the opprobrium the Guardians felt when unmarried pregnant women gave birth. Their main concern was that, by giving relief to this type of pauper, perhaps they were encouraging or aiding illegitimate births. In keeping with the double standards of the period, society felt that it was the woman's fault for getting pregnant, indicating a lack of morals on her part.

The Guardians sought advice on the subject on several occasions from the Poor Law Board as well as other neighbouring workhouse Guardians as to how they should deal with women 'of such bad habits'. Even Louise Twining, who was an enlightened

Victorian philanthropist who had done much work to improve the lives of paupers in the workhouses, had argued that maternity wards for unmarried women should be in the workhouse rather than a hospital so 'as to induce a proper sense of shame in the mothers'. (See Geoffrey Rivett's fascinating essay, also used above, at www.nhshistory.net.)

In June of 1897 the Guardians held a discussion about punishing the unfortunate woman in a way which would distinguish her from other 'deserving pauper women'. However, the matter was decided by the Poor Law Board itself. They had written a letter to the Guardians dated 5 March 1839 which said that it had been brought to their attention that in several union workhouses single, pregnant women were compelled to wear a dress of a peculiar colour, usually yellow, as a mark of disgrace. Fortunately, the Commissioners found that 'such distinction in dress or any equivalent mark of disgrace is inexpedient. Any attempt to inflict disgrace or punishment on the mother of a bastard, as such, appears to be in opposition to the principles which guided the legislature in the alteration of the law on this subject'.

In July 1896 one of the Guardians, Mr Blackburn, commented on the amount of feeble-minded women who lived in small villages who were brought to the workhouse with illegitimate babies. The stigma of giving birth whilst being unmarried impacted on everyone, and even respectable married women were sometimes mistakenly sent out of the workhouse just days from giving birth. One such experience was reported in February 1860 when 'A Poor Ratepayer' sent a letter to the editor of the local newspaper questioning why a young, married, pregnant servant had been ejected from Rotherham workhouse. The author of the letter relates that the unfortunate girl had been a former servant to the writer, had married and was deserted by her husband; she had returned to Rotherham, heavily pregnant, and was encouraged to go into the workhouse 'just for a month' in order to have her child. Reluctantly, she did so. Incredibly, days from giving birth she was turned out of this refuge as an 'unfit object of the charity'. The reason given was that she had a small amount of money which a 'gentleman workhouse official' had told her that she must surrender 'or go'.

The letter continued:

> The next morning [Thursday] she set off for Staffordshire with the hope of finding a distant relative of her father's to shelter her. She gave birth at six o'clock on the Saturday morning. This respectable woman only requested relief for the period of a month in an attempt to save her child but was refused this at the workhouse in Rotherham.

She had told the 'Poor Rate Payer' that 'eight women had been confined in the workhouse within the last two months and that six of them were unmarried and the child of one was by her father'. The following week the same Poor Rate Payer stated that the official had been the master of the workhouse (Mr George Bates) who had answered the charge by saying that he 'never to his knowledge saw the woman in his life'.

A similar case was reported in Sculcoates Union workhouse near Hull when another young woman was refused relief just a few weeks after its opening in 1844. She was 'rudely repulsed' after applying to the Guardians for relief. She told her story to a magistrate who ordered that she was to be accompanied by a police constable back to

THE ROTHERHAM WORKHOUSE.

TO THE EDITOR OF THE ADVERTISER.

Not having too much money, and having had to work hard for what I possess, I have acquired the habit of always expecting a pen'orth for my penny, and when I'm disappointed either in quantity or quality, by way of relief, I resolve either to have my "say" about it, or to spend no more pennies at that shop. Now, as in the case of poor-rates, I cannot adhere to this latter resolution, I have no alternative but to have my "say.

The master of the poor-house is pleased to contradict the plain, straightforward, truthful statement contained in your impression of the 11th instant, because, forsooth, he "never, to his knowledge, saw the woman in his life." Does his ignorance prove untruthfulness in my statement or neglect in the gentlemen officials?

If he, revelling in the bliss of ignorance, really disbelieves it, let me assure him that he is the only person in Rotherham who does; and shame upon his ungentlemanly contradiction, especially when he had made the wonderful discovery that it was the maid-servant's mistress and not her master who pleaded her cause. He might have reserved his flourishing small capitals and italics,—seeing there was no attempt made to conceal either person or gender—and his "palpable falsehood" also, for an effusion indicative of his ignorance. He might even have spared himself the trouble of replying at all, unless he had supplied the information asked for—*i.e.*, whether her child can be sheltered—who have the power to admit it—and who have the power to prevent its being turned out? She said the relieving officer turned her out, so why should the master "woman" her so hard? Is the supporter so much less worthy of respect than the supported? She was a respectable ratepayer, and hopes to be such again; she contributed her share towards supporting that institution which refused her relief in a time of great need; she added her toilings to those of the hard-working ratepayers who get their bread by the sweat of their brows, to uphold the dignity of the gentlemen officials, to support a table at which they fare sumptuously every day. She wished for the fare of half-boiled turnips and sour bread no longer than a month, yet even that was refused her; and why? Will a collector ever be refused, even if death and starvation meet him on the threshold? Then why should her very moderate claim have been refused?

Her friend said to her, "If you like I will go with you before the guardians, if you will wait till Monday." But her baby had to be born before Monday.

Now I have had my "say." I have a rate by me, £1 15s. 10d., which must be paid immediately, and the next time I make a claim I trust I may get it.

I am, Sir, yours respectfully,
A POOR RATE PAYER.

Rotherham, Feb. 22nd, 1860.

Letter from 'A Poor Rate Payer' (*RAMA*, 25 February 1860).

the workhouse to ensure that she was admitted – however, once again she was refused by a man named Marsh and 'driven from the door with reproachful insults' (Hull in Print, http://static.hullcc.gov.uk/hullinprint/archive/augsep2001/no_place_like.html). These cases indicate the censure which even married women received for being reduced to giving birth in the workhouse.

The Guardians felt that the cost of relief for unmarried women should be the responsibility of the putative father and much pressure was brought on the woman to name the man who had impregnated her. Throughout the Guardian's minutes are references to such children and enquiries were made to try to trace errant fathers. As early as July 1837, the medical officer was asked to look into the case of Joshua Robinson, 'a bastard child'. In September the same year it was ordered that an application be made to the Court of the Quarter Sessions for an order to be made upon George Wright for the maintenance of an illegitimate child 'born on the body of Ann Wade'. Very occasionally an agreement would be made about maintenance.

Such a curious arrangement was reached by the Guardians in September 1895 regarding the mother of the child, Mary Rosa, and the father of the illegitimate child, John Willie Hossell. The clerk produced an agreement which was carefully copied into the minutes and stated 'wherein John Willy Hossell and his mother Ann Hossell undertake jointly to pay 2/6 weekly until the illegitimate child is 14 years of age'. The clerk was instructed to file the agreement away for future reference.

Despite the problems facing married and unmarried mothers in the workhouse, it seems that the nursery of the Rotherham workhouse was nevertheless a comfortable place with a curious line in children's cots. A local newspaper reporter for the *Rotherham and Masbrough Advertiser* who visited the Rotherham workhouse nursery in April 1872 commented on:

> ...a 'wholesale rocking machine' which the nurse flatteringly described as a cradle capable of accommodating about a dozen children at a time. The construction had a considerable resemblance to swing boats at the fairs and in it were several chubby faced unfortunate children of unfortunate mothers who appeared to thoroughly enjoy the operation of rocking.

The children all had very a healthy appearance and the reporter noted they 'looked in every respect to be in more comfortable and happy circumstances than that class known as street Arabs'.

Nowhere is there portrayed a more popular image of the plight of workhouse children than in Charles Dickens' *The Adventures of Oliver Twist*. Even those people who have not read the book will be familiar, through musicals, films and plays, with that famous group of hungry workhouse children drawing lots to decide who will be the one to ask for more gruel whilst a group of Guardians feast at another table groaning with food. Dickens' subject stirred a climatic debate in local and national newspapers following the books serialisation in *Bentley's Miscellany* of 1837. The *Times* in particular led the debate about the abuses of the workhouse system, and the ill-treatment of paupers was regularly reported in its pages. The result of this media attention forced the Guardians (and the legislation of the time) to focus particularly on the dilemma of children in the workhouse. These were a group of paupers who were seen as being in the workhouse through no fault of their own and appeared to be treated with more sympathy by the Poor Law Commissioners; nevertheless, cruelty to children was regularly noted. The *Times* reported the case of the Fareham workhouse scandal, which involved three boys aged between four and five years of age. They were moved from Bishop Waltham workhouse to Fareham workhouse to go to school there. The workhouse master reported that they were healthy boys who had previously had problems with bed-wetting which disappeared after a few weeks at Bishop Waltham. Within days of being at Fareham, the boys were wetting and soiling their beds. The children were shamed for their 'dirty habits' and were put on half rations for two or three days a month. The schoolmistress grew concerned as they were becoming weak and ill. Eventually two of the boys, Robert Withers and Jonathon Cooke, were put in an outhouse with no heat. After ten days, with William

Warren, they were returned to Bishop Waltham in a covered cart. The master was shocked to find that they could not stand up or eat properly. The boys were nursed back to health, but Jonathon Cooke nearly died. The case was reported to the Poor Law Commissioners who investigated and found that Fareham workhouse was guilty of negligence. (www3.hants.gov.uk/museum/westbury-manor-museum/westbury-local-studies/fareham-workhouse.html)

In an attempt to try to get children out of the workhouse and away from evil influences from other inmates – which included their own parents – the Guardians and the Poor Law legislators developed many schemes. The Rotherham Guardians, as in other workhouses, had an apprenticeship scheme where pauper children were sent out to work in the homes and workshops of local traders. This would enable them to learn a trade and 'not to be a burden on the ratepayers of Rotherham'. Traditionally these children were offered to employers for a small sum, such as £5; the scheme was open to anyone who would take a child off the parish's hands. The Rotherham apprenticeship scheme had been criticised by one of the Guardians in 1880 who stated that 'there was a disposition to apprentice the children without due regard to their position during their servitude' and often children were sent to the first place who offered to take them (*RAMA*, 25 December 1880).

A case of the ill-treatment of a child apprenticed into service was investigated by the Sheffield Guardians in September 1859. A young girl named Mary Ann Hogg had been sent out of the Sheffield workhouse and placed in the service of a Mrs Cox, who was described as an Irishwomen with a 'whinging and hypocritical manner'. The girl was found to have been badly beaten. The reporter revealed that her head had been covered with injuries from being beaten with a coal rake. There were large swellings on the back of her ears, blood on her neck and shoulders and on the left side of her back and her arm, evidence of very severe blows. The woman was castigated by the chair of the Guardians, who stated that if the girl had been injured more seriously he would have taken her before the magistrates. If the girl had been disobedient she should have been returned to the house. It was agreed that Mary Ann would be returned to the care of the Guardians and it was reported that Mrs Cox left the room sobbing.

In June 1873 an enquiry was received by the Rotherham Guardians from Forest Gate District School, in Essex, informing them that their training ship *Goliath* was now in a satisfactory condition and they had vacancies for boys. These were ships requested by the Poor Law Board from the Lords of the Admiralty for 'the training of pauper boys'. A further request was made in December 1900 regarding any boys aged from thirteen to sixteen who would be suitable for training for seamanship on the training ship *Exmouth*. The Guardians approved of this kind of training, which would give the boys 'a future career serving in the Merchant or Royal Navy'.

But it seems that the most successful scheme to remove children from the workhouse at Rotherham was the 'boarding out scheme' – although initially it did not get off to a very good start. In December 1870 the Poor Law Board sent the Guardians details about a new initiative from the Boarding Out Commission. (Boarding out was a scheme whereby children would be taken out of the workhouse and fostered by local working-class families for a small payment.) They sent out letters dated 3 April 1871

SHEFFIELD GUARDIANS' MEETING.

CRUELTY TO A PAUPER CHILD.

The Board of Guardians held their weekly meeting on Wednesday. Ald. Saunders, the chairman, presided; and Messrs. Youdan, Crawshaw, Leonard, Watkinson, and Hodgkinson were also present.

Cruelty to a Sheffield pauper apprentice girl (*RJ*, 19 September 1859).

stating the terms of the boarding out scheme to the churchwardens and clergymen of the different parishes. The Guardians requested that boarding out committees be developed for:

> Orphans and deserted boys and girls between the ages of 2–10 years and having also appointed a committee for carrying the same into effect… to communicate to them the names and addresses of any recommendable fit person in your parish who may be desirous of taking children into their homes on the terms adverted to viz: on being allowed 3/- per week for board and lodgings, 10/- a quarter for clothing, the school pence or fees, the attendance of the union medical officer in case of sickness or accident and the funeral expenses on the event of death… It was recommended that the child should be brought up as one of their own and will provide it with proper food, lodgings and washing and endeavour to train it in habits of truthfulness, obedience, personal cleanliness and industry.

The letters which were sent out proved very successful and it was not long before replies started pouring in. Revd John Cox (Kimberworth) promised to give the matter his full attention, as did Revd C. Hayes (West Melton) and Revd W. Stothert (Thorpe Hesley). The success of the boarding out scheme was brought to the attention of the board in October 1879 when one of the Guardians, Mr Huntsman, asked the relieving officer, Mr Dawson, how the scheme was progressing, as 'it was desirable to clear the house of children'. He was informed by Mr Dawson that the scheme had gone 'really well'. However, only two years later the scheme seemed to have collapsed as when Mr Moseley, the Inspector of Workhouse Schools, asked how many boarded out children there were in the union in January 1881 he was told that there were 'no cases in this union'.

Despite its shaky beginning, a further attempt at the boarding out scheme was tried again in Rotherham in November 1883 when Earl Fitzwilliam proposed (seconded by Mr Eyre) that once again a circular letter be sent to each clergyman in the area to form a boarding out committee. This second attempt was more successful. In January 1887 the Revd F. Freeman, who was on the boarding out committee for Wickersley, inserted a letter in the local press regarding the case of two boarded out children who were in the choir of his parish aged eleven and twelve years of age. He stated that they were boarded with a respectable widow and said that 'if the Guardians saw them in their clean choir clothes and heard them sing they could but be pleased with them. No one would think that they were connected in any way with the union workhouse.' (*RAMA*, 17 November 1888.) However, he does criticise the Guardians for the low rate of pay for clothing and food of these boarded out children. A further discussion took place in the board room regarding the boarding out of these children with relatives as to whether they should they be paid the same rate as the other foster carers, and the Guardians agreed that this should be allowed.

The scheme was not always successful, however, and some foster parents who had been recommended did not quite come up to scratch. The local newspaper reported that two boarded out children had been living with a Mr and Mrs William Dyer (who lived on Wortley Road, Rotherham). It was brought to the Guardians' attention that Mr Dyer had been 'brought before the justices and fined for being drunk', and it was requested that these two children, John Clark and William Brooks, be returned back to the workhouse. During the investigations it turned out that Mr Dyer was also guilty of bigamy and the Guardians were not happy that the boarding out committee had approved the placement. A petition was sent to the Guardians from some of the neighbours of the Dyers stating that they were 'the proper people to take care of the children'. Revd Carr, chair of the Kimberworth boarding out committee, sent a letter to the Guardians requesting that the children remain, as they were completely settled and very affectionate towards the foster parents. The Guardians considered it, but when Revd Blazeby pointed out 'anyone who had been once or twice the worse for liquor was unfit to take care of the children', it was ordered that the children return to the workhouse.

On 26 May 1884 a letter was received from the same Revd Carr resigning his own position as chair – accompanied by the notices of the whole Kimberworth boarding out committee *en masse*. In his letter, Carr stated that the Guardians had 'virtually set aside the authority of this committee', and added that 'the characters of both these people were thoroughly gone into before our consideration was approved'. (*RAMA*, 31 May 1884.) As a consequence of this action there was no longer a boarding out committee in Kimberworth, so it was moved and seconded that all the children boarded out in the area be withdrawn. The relieving officers were instructed that the ten children in the scheme were to be based in any districts where boarding out committees still existed.

One of the more popular schemes that the Guardians used was the 'cottage homes scheme'. As early as May 1873, a letter addressed to Mr Stansfield, the president of the Local Government Board, suggested the scheme, best described as 'a village in which the children might be distributed, leading as nearly as may be the lives of the best class of cottager's children'. By September 1899 the attention of the Guardians was brought to the recommendations of the select committee of the House of Commons for the provision of cottage homes. The recommendations were that 'all children other than infants should be provided for outside of the workhouse premises'. It was agreed that houses owned by the Guardians in Alma Road would be suitable to be fitted for the reception of children in these cottage homes, but first there was the small matter of getting the existing tenants out of the houses. There might have been some difficulty getting the tenants out as it was not until June 1901 when a committee of Guardians was formed to visit the cottage homes in Sheffield and Eccleshall and report back that the subject appeared to be taken more seriously. The committee were unanimous in the praise for these establishments and recommended the removal of children from the body of the workhouse and into the properties as soon as possible. It was agreed that:

> The villa properties in Alma Road be adapted for the use of the workhouse children as a residence under properly qualified officials as trainers and caretakers under the management of the master and matron of the workhouse. Its children will have no connection what so ever with the adult inmates of the workhouse, but the food, clothing and other necessaries to be provided from the stores of the workhouse as at present. The children for school and church attendances go directly from the home and not through the general entrance and the clerk be instructed to deal legally with the present tenants in order that the scheme may be put into execution as early as practicable.

With the sanction of the Local Government Board it was agreed that a boys' and girls' attendant would be elected for the role, and James Nichols appeared before the Guardians in July 1901 and was duly elected. It was agreed that his salary would be £25 p.a., increasing by £2 10s annually to a maximum of £30 (with board, apartment, laundry, uniform and medical attention and 1s a week in lieu of beer). In June 1902, the minutes record that the clerk received twenty-three applications for foster mothers in connection with the cottage homes. These were sent to the House and Finance committee for their consideration, and in August 1902 two women were appointed. Unfortunately, we have no details regarding these foster mothers as the only mention is that the minutes of the House and Finance committee meetings were 'accepted in their entirety'. Later that year, in October 1902, it was decided that the lady Guardians and lady visitors would take on the responsibility for visiting and inspecting the children in the cottage homes, and report any problems back to the Board of Guardians.

These cottage homes would be the precursor of such smaller home-like buildings as the Sunshine Homes or the Cheshire homes where children were accommodated under the watchful eye of a matron or foster parents. The idea was to have a more familial role and in this they were quite successful. The removal of the children from the workhouse was seen as desirable and these schemes resulted in a reduction of the numbers of workhouse inmates. However, another pauper group was beginning to escalate in size: the unfortunate people deemed by the Victorians to be 'lunatics and imbeciles'.

eight

Lunatics and Imbeciles

One of the biggest problems facing the medical officers and the Guardians of Rotherham was the increasing amount of people who were unable to gain employment and leave the workhouse. This was the class of people with varying degrees of mental impairments, who contributed to the overcrowding in Rotherham workhouse, a subject which was increasingly listed in the minutes. The most harmless of this class were given simple tasks if they were capable and were classed as 'imbeciles'. Previous to the Poor Law Acts these poor souls were lodged in the community and were labelled as 'village idiots': as a result, they were possibly more protected and indulged by the community at large. Once they came into the workhouse they were isolated, and I would suggest feared, as certainly the needs of this class of pauper was the most misunderstood.

Those type of inmates who were classified as lunatics could remain in the workhouse as long as they were considered to be harmless, but the more severe or dangerous types were sent to the local asylums. Paupers of this class were usually sent to the South Yorkshire Asylum at Wadsley, near Sheffield, or to the Wakefield Asylum. These asylums came under the jurisdiction of both the Poor Law Board and the Commission for Lunacy (who regularly visited the asylums as well as the Rotherham workhouse and made reports on their findings to the Guardians). The Guardians were aware that both these classes of paupers needed more specialist care and supervision than the workhouse officials were able to offer, but they didn't know what the solution was. Where possible, the Guardians would send the lunatic pauper inmates to other asylums. The Rotherham Guardians would then be responsible for the patient's maintenance and care.

Regular inspections of the lunatic wards in the Rotherham workhouse were held by the Inspectors of the Commissioners for Lunacy, and in November 1862 they drew the attention of the Guardians to the fact that there was no receiving ward for lunatics at the workhouse. It seems that these unfortunate people were scattered with the different classes of other paupers, and three years later it was noted that no separate accommodation was yet available for the imbeciles. The Poor Law Board in February 1865 sent a letter to the Guardians enquiring if a separate room could be provided for 'nameless idiots' as they were at present lodged with more dangerous lunatics.

A complaint was made by the Poor Law inspector in September 1870. He noted that:

> Two violent lunatics named David Taylor and Hugh Hunt were in bed in this ward and two sane paupers were looking after them. The lunatics are detained until there is room in an asylum when they will be removed. The two attendant paupers were old and partially infirm men, quite unable to exert any effective control, but the master said they were the two best qualified men he had in the house. There are no padded rooms and no proper baths for imbeciles. On the female side of the house, there is no imbecile ward though a room is now used by day and by night for a few of the worst cases of this description.

Stung by the remarks from the Commissioner for Lunacy, it was decided in September 1870 that when the workhouse was enlarged better facilities and extra wards would be provided at the workhouse – and it was agreed that a padded room would be added for the more dangerous lunatics. They replied to the Commissioners that:

> With respect to the lunatics the Guardians desire to act on the plan of removing them at once from their own residences to the asylum when the proper steps for such purpose have been taken and it is only general when there is no immediate admission to be had for them in an asylum that they are temporarily removed to the union house...A padded room for both sexes will be provided. The old paupers looking after the lunatics Taylor and Hunt although not able to exert much control over them themselves were with easy call of the porter at his lodge close by. The Guardians have not before required providing padded rooms for imbeciles. Baths can be easily procured when required.

It seems that the Guardians took the report regarding the accommodation for this type of paupers very seriously indeed and only a month later in November 1870 plans for two wards, one for male lunatics and one for female lunatics, with a separate padded room was approved by the Guardians and forwarded to the Poor Law Board. Once the enlargements were completed in May 1872 and the new lunatic wards of the Rotherham workhouse were opened they were described in glowing terms by a local reporter. He described the new wards as:

> ...the most complete arrangements were found for the proper care and safety of unfortunate and imbecile humanity. There are two rooms set apart for these cases, one of males and the other for females. The fire places are enclosed in strong iron grating and the windows are similarly guarded. There is also a padded room where dangerous lunatics are confined and the fittings are so complete as to wholly to prevent any inmate from injuring themselves. The walls to a considerable height are covered in vulcanised India rubber thickly padded and in segments. These are locked to the wall in strong casing but can be removed with considerable ease for the purpose of cleaning, and the floor is covered with a thick bed. Apertures are made in the door to enable them who are in charge to see whether the patient is attempting any violence upon himself and whenever this room is occupied there is a man constantly in attendance. (*RAMA*, 27 May 1872.)

SUICIDE OF A FEMALE AT THE WORKHOUSE.

On Wednesday evening last Henry Badger, Esq., deputy coroner, and a respectable jury, held an inquest on the body of Elizabeth Gilling, who had destroyed her life when under the influence of insanity. It appeared that after the sitting of the Board of Guardians on Monday last, a request was made to the proper officers for the admission of the deceased into the Workhouse as a lunatic, her friends being fearful of her committing suicide, or otherwise injuring herself. The deceased was therefore placed in the lying-in ward of the house, in consequence of the usual ward being occupied.

Mr. George Gilling, farmer, Brookhouse, identified the body in the lying-in room as his wife. He said she was brought to the Workhouse at his request on Monday last, as he could not attend to her. She had been in a low desponding state of mind for some time. He intended to contribute to her support. In March last she told him she had tried to hang herself, and since then he had constantly watched her, or had some one with her. She had avoided him one night, and slipped out; he then went in search of her, and found her on her hands and knees in a ditch bottom, among some thorns. He had not the slightest doubt that she had come to her death by her own hand. The deceased had been under medical advice for some time.

Sarah Hutchinson (one of the inmates of the workhouse) said the deceased, Elizabeth Gilling, came into the house on Monday last, and was placed in the lying-in ward. She believed her to be insane. Witness slept in the same room with her. On Monday and Tuesday nights she appeared very restless, and paced a good deal about the room. On Tuesday night deceased went to bed apparently the same as usual. At two o'clock in the morning she came to her (witness's) bedside, and said she could not sleep; she said she had not been out of bed before. On that occasion deceased smoked a pipe; afterwards she got into bed and stayed there till five o'clock; she then came again to witness's bedside, and told her she could not sleep. At about half-past five she heard a strange noise from deceased's bed, and found she had cut her throat. Dr. Hardwicke was at once sent for, but before he arrived she was dead. Witness was not aware of any knife being about the room when she went to bed; the door of the bedroom was kept locked, the key being inside. Deceased had told her she had once attempted to hang herself, and had hurt her neck in doing so. In witness's opinion deceased was in a very low and desponding state of mind.

Mary Linley, another inmate, gave very similar evidence.

Sarah Barker, nurse at the Workhouse, said she saw deceased on the previous night about nine o'clock. She then detailed how she was aroused on the morning by the previous witnesses. She at once sent for Dr. Hardwicke, but when he arrived she was dead. Dr. Hardwicke found the knife produced by the side of deceased on the bed; she did not have it to her dinner; it was one of three witness kept in her private room in a drawer. She could not swear all three of the knives were in the drawer the previous night, nor was she aware that deceased was in her room at all the previous day. Deceased had said she had a good husband. Witness believed she had committed the act herself.

Suicide of a female lunatic at the Rotherham workhouse (*RJ*, 10 July 1858).

The new wards had impressed the reporter, but there is still no mention of any one person to care for or supervise the patients on a regular basis: this role was undertaken, as always, by other paupers of the workhouse, and it was therefore inevitable that tragic accidents would happen. In July 1858 an item was included in the *Rotherham and Masbrough Advertiser* regarding the suicide of a female in the Rotherham workhouse. It stated that, on Wednesday evening last, Henry Badger Esq., the deputy coroner, had held an inquest on the body of Elisabeth Gilling, an inmate who had destroyed her life whilst under the influence of insanity. The reporter noted that on Monday last, a request was made to the proper officers for the admission of the deceased into the workhouse as a lunatic. The deceased was placed in the lying-in ward of the workhouse as a consequence of the usual ward being occupied. After two sleepless nights a witness (who shared the same room with her) heard a strange noise from the deceased's bed and found she had cut her throat with a knife. The deceased was described as being 'in a very low and despondent state of mind'. The medical officer, Dr Hardwick, had been sent for but the woman was dead before he arrived. The jury returned a verdict of 'temporary insanity'.

So it must have come as a relief when the Guardians were informed that the Wadsley Asylum was now open for the reception of lunatics, commencing on 21 August 1872. The asylum offered generous terms to the local workhouses, stating that the charge for paupers of the West Riding would be 10s 6d per week (and for other unions it would be 14s a week). A deputation of Rotherham Guardians had been invited to visit on the 7 August to inspect the asylum and they reported back very favourably to the board.

The costs of keeping the lunatics in the workhouse and in the local asylums were spiralling to such an extent that in September 1874 the government, to ease the costs, agreed to pay 4s towards the maintenance for each of the lunatics kept at other asylums and paid for by the Guardians. It was noted the following month that, for the maintenance of lunatics at Wadsley, the amount paid by the Guardians up to the previous midsummer was £320 16s 6d. From that amount, they received £108 12s from the government.

In August 1879 an anonymous account was published in the local newspaper describing what life was like inside Wadsley Asylum, under the heading of an 'Interesting Narrative by a Cured Patient'. He describes the attendants, 'who bids us cease in a loud tone and if not obeyed at once you are handled very rudely, pushed backwards and on occasions punched in the ribs'. He describes an incident where he threw an object at an attendant:

> I was laid hold of by two or three men and banged first against a wall and then a floor. If you make your mind up to report the attendants to the doctors, the attendant will not give you a chance to speak. You are then locked up in a dark room for as much as 12 hours. Patients who are recovering are used as servants. (*RAMA*, 16 August 1879)

A very similar case was investigated at Chesterfield when it was reported that a 'ward man' and a deaf and dumb child were in charge of the imbecile ward when the dead body of William Bennett, aged forty-four years old, was found to have a broken arm. The ward man, Joseph Stones, stated that he had found the dead body between two beds, but his story was refuted by another inmate, William Lock, who said that he had heard the sound of a body falling to the floor after Stones had gone into the room. The surgeon was called. He questioned William Lock, who told him that Stones had frequently ill-used the deceased. Lock said he had witnessed the deceased man being beaten with a stick until he called out 'murder'. He had witnessed Stones giving the deceased many blows with his fists. He had also seen Stones taking soiled linen from a bed and beating an inmate about the head with it. Mr Bluett, the surgeon, stated that both bones of the left arm were broken in a very suspicious manner and the matter was adjourned until the post-mortem could be held.

Meanwhile, back in Rotherham, it was becoming increasingly obvious that by now Wadsley was getting very overcrowded. By August 1883 a letter from a visiting magistrate was sent to the Guardians stating that the asylum at Wadsley was

BRUTAL TREATMENT OF AN IMBECILE AT THE CHESTERFIELD WORKHOUSE.

On Tuesday, Mr Busby, coroner, held an inquest at the Chesterfield Workhouse, on the body of a man named Wm. Bennett, who died on Saturday last, aged forty-four years, under the following circumstances:—Wm. Lock, a painter, and an inmate of the house, said—On Monday week I was in the imbecile ward, and about ten minutes to six in the morning, the wardsman, Joseph Stones, passed my bed to go to where deceased was sleeping. He at once commenced cursing deceased and said, "Oh! here's a mess." In about a minute after I heard a scume, and something like a person falling, and Stones continued swearing. He called to me to go to him, but I did not answer. He called again and I went, and Stones said, "Look here, the man's head is cut." I said, "Yes, it's the old game again." The deceased was sitting on the ground near to the entrance of the room, and until Stones went in there was nobody else in the room but deceased and a deaf and dumb boy. The other inmates generally got up at half-past five. The nurse went to deceased, and presently she came to the door with Stones, and he said deceased's arm was broken, so I said he had better send for the doctor. Mr Bluett, the surgeon, came, and he asked me how the deceased's arm was broken, and I repeated to him what I had heard and seen. Stones first said deceased had done it in the pump yard on Saturday, then that he had done it in the night, and afterwards that he had fallen out of bed. I have frequently seen the deceased ill-used in the imbecile ward by Stones. I have seen him beaten with a stick until he has called out "Murder," and I have seen blows given to him with the fist. I have also seen the soiled linen taken from the bed and beaten about the man's head. When I have spoken to the wardsman about ill-treating the deceased he has said it was the master's orders, and that he was to rub deceased's nose in the dirt. There are other cases of ill-treatment in the same ward. Stones is not an imbecile; he has charge of the imbecile ward. Deceased, I am of opinion, received the wound on the head and the injuries to the arm in the scuffle.—Mr Bluett, surgeon, said: On examining deceased I found both bones of the left arm were broken; in fact, the arm was twisted up to form something like another elbow. I found a wound on the head which penetrated to the skull. I asked Stones how it had happened, and he said he did not know—that he found deceased between the two beds, with his arm doubled up under him. My suspicions were first aroused by the little deaf and dumb boy, who was very excited whilst I was in the room. He took hold of my sleeve and pulled me to the fire place, and imitated a person inflicting blows and groaning. He is a very intelligent little boy. Deceased died on Saturday morning from exhaustion, caused by the injuries supervening on an already emaciated frame.—The Coroner adjourned the inquiry for a week, in order that a post-mortem examination should be made.

Brutal treatment of an imbecile at Chesterfield workhouse (*RAMA*, 7 March 1868).

overcrowded. It requested that the Guardians send 'non but the most urgent cases'. Pressure was mounting, and in November 1891 the Guardians received a letter from the medical superintendent at Wadsley stating that due to demands on the female side, it would be necessary for them to discharge some of the quieter, harmless cases back to the workhouse. Unfortunately, however, there was no room at the Rotherham workhouse either, and the clerk was instructed to write to the asylum stating that 'due to building enlargements there is no accommodation at this moment'.

Despite the enlargements, by July 1889 it seems that the Rotherham Guardians had made no special arrangements for the care of those paupers classed as 'imbeciles'. These 'harmless lunatics' were patients who were unable to do any but the simplest tasks and their vast numbers meant that they were unable to be supervised properly. As many as possible were sent to Wadsley, but after studying yet another letter from Dr Kay, the superintendent of Wadsley, regarding his inability to take any more harmless lunatics in October 1894, the medical officer for Rotherham, Dr Robinson, was instructed to examine the harmless lunatics in the Rotherham workhouse and to give his report to the Guardians on the situation. He wrote:

> I therefore think that if the board entertains increasing the already large number of imbeciles, a special building should be erected for their reception with two paid attendants, one for male and one for females. It is impossible for me to be responsible for their safety without proper precautions. Not very long ago one of these harmless cases fell off a high wall and broke his leg and in two months died as a result of his injuries. At the Coroner's inquest the officials of the workhouse were placed in a very invidious position.

It seems that there was no room for this class of pauper anywhere. Once again, on the 19 January 1895 the case of harmless lunatics was brought to the attention of the Guardians by the Poor Law Authorities. They stated that these persons should not be confined in ordinary lunatic asylums, especially in the overcrowded wards of the present asylums. Alternatively the present arrangement of keeping them in separate wards in association with some inmates of the workhouse 'is most undesirable'. The Guardians, after a long discussion on what should be done for this class of pauper, wrote back to the Poor Law Board that the Guardians 'are of the opinion that separate institutions should be provided for where they may be beneficially occupied and receive training suitable for their special condition and the cost should not fall exclusively on the rate payers but should be provided for from Imperial taxation'.

The Rotherham Guardians sent out circular letters outlining the above proposition to all the 642 unions in England and Wales. The difficulties of categorising this class of inmate was outlined by one of the Guardians, a Mr Cox, who stated that some of these harmless patients were sane for periods and for that reason, they should not be sent to asylums. But at the same time, the mixing of the harmless lunatics with the rest of the workhouse population was not desirable. The Guardians noted that the habits of some of these patients were objectionable and the effects that this had on the young was detrimental and injurious.

The West Riding County Council were sympathetic but they were still endeavouring to pressurise the Guardians into having separate wards at the workhouse and special attendants for the better supervision of these paupers. They also requested that the Guardians provide at least two wards for the separation of the sexes. The Guardians talked about the costs of maintaining these cases at Wadsley. One of the Guardians, Mr Blackburn, pointed out that there were 180 harmless lunatics who were chargeable to the Rotherham Guardians already at Wadsley. It seems that the Guardians decided to resolve the problem by appropriating a new block in order to provide accommodation specifically for this class of pauper. They wrote to the Poor Law Board for the sanction for this. A reply from them stated that the board could offer no objection to the proposed appropriation of the new block for the use of the harmless lunatics received into the Rotherham workhouse under the provision of Section 25 of the Lunacy Act 1890. It had been decided that male and female lunatic attendants were to be appointed to supervise this class of pauper. In November 1901, Mr J.A. Russell and his wife were appointed.

Today there is a natural aversion to labelling any child with mental health problems, but during the period of study, young children were being sent to the local asylums. A prime example of this was Mildred Hall, a girl of six described as a 'harmless lunatic' who had been admitted to Wadsley Asylum on 1 July 1895. Due to the overcrowding, the Guardians decided that she was to be sent to Royal Albert Asylum in Lancaster. The number of asylums now specialising in the treatment of children was increasing, and a part of Wakefield Asylum named Stanley Hall was a place where 'idiot' children could be sent. In February 1901 the Guardians were informed that Charles Albert Stone and John Peter Conroy had been removed to Stanley Hall for more specialised treatment. These asylums believed that children with learning difficulties could be educated and found some kind of employment, so were very revolutionary in their outlook.

There were a few occasions when the Guardians requested that children be returned back to the workhouse at Rotherham if the Guardians felt that the specialised treatment was being ineffective. A letter regarding the cases of Edgar Bray and Emily Lewis was received from the Royal Albert Asylum asking that their removal be deferred until the beginning of July 1901. It seems that Edgar Bray had made some progress during his stay as a further letter was received by the Guardians from Mr Bray (the father of Edgar) asking that his son be allowed to stay at the Royal Albert. The clerk was asked to write to the secretary of the asylum and make enquires as to his progress and his daily activities, but it seems that his progress had been minimal. In June 1902, the two children were returned back to the workhouse.

The treatment of these types of paupers was not high on the list of priorities for the Guardians. Being kept in wards with other paupers would add to the deterioration in their behaviour. Many were used in the hospital wards as attendants (and no doubt other positions within the workhouse also) and the use of this type of pauper led the Guardians into cases of mismanagement and allegations of malfeasance at the Rotherham workhouse.

nine

Mismanagement and Allegations at the Workhouse

It was inevitable that the Rotherham Board of Guardians would be held up to public enquiry on a fairly regular basis. The Guardians had enormous power and status within the workhouse system, whilst at the same time dealing with huge amounts of ratepayer's money in the form of relief. One of the most frequent accusations was that there was no fixed amount of relief paid: much of it was down to the discretion of the relieving officers themselves. Any accusations or allegations about officers of the workhouse had to be reported to the Poor Law Board and investigated with the utmost levels of integrity. As time went on these accusations became more frequent. The Guardians insisted that some issues would not be discussed in front of the local newspaper reporters; instead, they would be discussed in a committee from which the press would be excluded. However, the reality was that, as often as not, details were leaked out to the press and commented on the following week.

The power that the officers had over the pauper inmates was absolute in this period: the poor 'knew their place' and the concept of class structure was ingrained in the workhouse system. Incidents of abuse were frequent, although initially such accusations were dealt with within the Guardians' board meetings. However, when the complaints spread around the town the Guardians had to request an investigation by the Poor Law inspectors, who in turn often felt that the only way of dealing with the allegations was at a public enquiry. It has to be said that the Guardians did not exactly come out of most of these enquires with their credibility intact; in addition, the minutes indicate that some issues were certainly not explained as fully as they should have been.

The first rumblings of mismanagement to end in a public enquiry were heard in December 1871 when an anonymous letter was sent to the Board of Guardians. The letter suggested that the amount of relief and extras (usually alcoholic) given to the paupers of Rotherham was higher than any other local workhouse. The Guardians decided that as the letter was unsigned they should ignore it. The anonymous sender(s) then followed up with a letter to the local newspaper, the *Rotherham and Masbrough Advertiser*, once again outlining their concerns about the abuse of the ratepayer's money. The authors of the letter, in order to be taken seriously and to make themselves known to the editor, this time included their signatures. They were: Mr Robert Henry Sharp, a local coal merchant residing in Moorgate; J. Brown Junior; W.H. Gummer; Joseph Wells; and Mr Charles Morris (*RAMA*, 6 January 1872).

The Local Government Board was well aware of the issues around the amount of relief and in particular the amount of 'extras' given, and, as we have seen, had previously sent letters to the Guardians drawing their attention to the fact that Rotherham workhouse had the largest amount of relief paid out in the county. In January 1872, following the allegations in the local press, they requested a report on this matter to be sent to them by the next Guardians' board meeting day. The vice chair to the Guardians, Alderman John Guest, was requested to reply to the Poor Law inspector, Mr R. Basil Cane, which he did on 16 January 1872. A copy of the actual letter is preserved in the back of the Board of Guardian's minutes for the period June 1869-March 1872. Alderman Guest informed Mr Cane that:

> There have been weeks when outdoor relief has exceeded the amount distributed in corresponding weeks... but a comparison of corresponding weeks in other years is not a reliable guide or test insomuch as in some weeks payments for extras supplied during the quarter which swell the amount in other ways than for actual relief given... namely funerals, clothing, cod liver oil, shoes, spirits, wine etc.

Mr Cane had compared Rotherham's costs of relief with other unions in the South Yorkshire area. As Alderman Guest pointed out, these comparisons did not serve any purpose because of the different industries of the local towns. He pointed out that Keighley, for example, was totally different from Rotherham, 'insomuch as a considerable part of this union consists of large iron works and very extensive collieries and therefore more chance of accidents happening and consequently more chance of pauper families being brought into the workhouse as a result'. However, Alderman Guest did admit some errors of judgement, 'namely [that] during the mismanagement of the late master and matron (Mr and Mrs Mitchell) the Guardians had not exercised due vigilance with respect to the stock and the state of the clothing'. When the new master had taken over, the stock was found to be 'very insufficient in quantity and as unfit for use as to require a considerable immediate outlay'. Despite this lapse, the Guardians declared that they would make:

> No decision to do otherwise than render the fullest explanation in every respect in their power and are thankful to have their attention drawn to any excess (exceptional or otherwise) which may be found in their expenditure of the funds of the union. The remedying of such cases being more important to them than any thing else. They can fairly take credit for regular and assiduous attention to their duties imposed on them... and by their relieving officers to the care brought before them and a sufficiently vigorous

> administration of the affairs of the union exercised by them in this judicial accordance with the peculiar character and requirements of this district.

Alderman Guest concluded that the Rotherham Guardians were happy to open a full public investigation if Mr Cane felt that it was necessary. Meanwhile, in April of the same year, the Local Government Board requested that the Guardians send them the returns of the quantity and costs of spirits and ale for the year ending Michaelmas 1871 – and consequently it was decided that Mr Cane would indeed hold an enquiry into the allegations. It appears from the minutes that Mr Cane had requested certain 'information' from Mr Sharp (the coal merchant who wrote the letter of complaint mentioned above), who then wrote back stating that he was concerned that Mr Cane might not be given access to all the books and evidence which he would need. Mr Cane replied on 22 April 1872:

> An Inspector has ample legal power to call for and if necessary to compel the production of books, papers and documents necessary to the enquiry and they could not be withheld from him as you seem to anticipate they might be at Rotherham union. All persons accused have a right to know who their accusers are and to be provided with complete particulars of the charges against themselves when called upon to do so by competent authority. Having given you this explanation I again invite you to send me the information asked for in my letter of the 3rd instant.

There is no clue in the minutes to identify what information Mr Cane was asking for, but Mr Sharp curiously responded to the letter by stating that 'in reply to your last note we beg to decline furnishing you with the details that you request for previously explained reasons'. (In light of later events, this was possibly because he was not to liberty to disclose his sources.)

The local newspaper took up the cudgels, and it was reported in June 1872 that considerable dissatisfaction had been expressed by numbers of ratepayers as to the management of the Rotherham workhouse. They were grateful that Mr Robert Henry Sharp had undertaken the task of responsibility of voicing their grievances (*RAMA*, 15 June 1872). Despite this public concern, without the co-operation of Mr Sharp, Mr Cane would be unable to proceed any further: the Guardians were no doubt congratulating themselves that they had avoided public scrutiny into these matters. However, the issues became such a matter for public debate in the local press that a letter was received by the Guardians from Mr Cane (dated 17 June 1872) stating that he felt that question needed to be open to public scrutiny. He informed the Guardians that he would be holding a public enquiry on the 22 June 1872. Alderman Guest attended the initial stages of the enquiry – and he appeared to be worried by it, as on his return he suggested to the Guardians at the next board meeting day that a 'professional man' be engaged to represent the Guardians. However, the other Guardians felt that it was unnecessary at this time (though it was noted that the press would be in attendance at the enquiry).

When Mr Sharp was finally asked to give the public enquiry the details of his complaints about the Guardians' mismanagement, he listed a range of grievances, including some new allegations. Firstly, he complained that a number of pigs belonging to one of the Guardians, Mr Hollins, had been kept at the workhouse 'at the ratepayers' expense'. When asked who gave him this information, he refused to give the person's name, as he stated that he was given the information in confidence. He mentioned that there had also been fowl kept at the workhouse, which he noted had been got rid of prior to the enquiry as also being the private property of the Guardians. He further stated that some of the Guardians were getting cream from the workhouse and not paying for it, but once again he refused to give their names. He finally went on to say that, in the opinion of the group, that there was an excessive cost of relief paid out to the Rotherham workhouse patients and those outdoor patients of the town in the form of medical extras. Mr Cane said that the Guardians had stated that the high local costs arose from 'a greater price being given [for goods] than in other neighbouring towns', although they gave no evidence for this. Mr Sharp also complained that he felt the Guardians were the 'judges of destitution' as the relieving officers could pay out relief of either 2s or 5s at their own discretion. Naturally Mr Cane wanted evidence of this, and asked that Mr Sharp provide this evidence. In order to do so, Mr Sharp was given access to the workhouse books and accounts and the enquiry was adjourned until he had chance to obtain the details that he needed for the enquiry to be properly investigated (*RAMA*, 21 June 1872).

The Guardians also had to gather their own evidence for the next public enquiry, which was finally arranged to be held over four days (from 5 October to 12 October 1872). A solicitor was engaged to act for the Guardians. Indeed, a copy of the newspaper report of the proceedings is kept in the back of the minute book for June 1869-May 1872. Mr Sharp and his cohorts had been asked by Mr Cane to submit a list of allegations detailing the mismanagement of the Guardians of Rotherham. Mr Sharp submitted the following issues, once again adding new ones, which were:

> That pigs, the private property of a Guardian, have been fed at the workhouse and sold by him thence direct to butchers.
>
> That it has been the constant practice for certain officials of the workhouse to send there for cream and sundry other articles without payment altogether or at nominal charge.
>
> That very numerous and serious deviation from the plans of the fever wards were made at the cost of the ratepayer.
>
> That no wash houses were originally built in connection with the fever wards which, when added, were built without having being submitted to public competition.

For the first part of the allegation it would seem that the pigs belonged to a previous Guardian who no longer lived in the town, who had them driven them up to the workhouse in July 1870 and instructed the porter, Thomas Straw, to put them down to 'Mr John Brown'. The porter said that the pigs were taken out in September 1870 by this same man. The clerk to the Guardians, Mr Barrass, was next called and he said that he was aware of the pigs. He said that due to concerns about the meat which had been delivered to the workhouse, it was agreed that pigs be kept. However, if the pigs had been supplied for the paupers it is unclear why they were removed. The clerk to the Rotherham Guardians was asked if he was aware of the pigs being kept at the workhouse and he agreed that he had known about it. He also commented that the pigs were affected with all sorts of diseases, 'including lunacy' (to which there was much laughter), but he agreed that 'sending the pigs in to the workhouse were an injudicious thing to do'.

The second point which Mr Sharp had alleged was investigated. It appeared that the matron, Mrs Turner, was in the habit of selling off surplus milk and cream from the workhouse. She stated that the money was given to the master to be declared to the clerk and the Guardians on board day. At the time this allegation was made, the inmates of the workhouse were given old milk which was listed in the provisions to the workhouse. A tender for milk from May 1872 gives a price of 11d a gallon for new milk and 4d a gallon for old milk. Interestingly, on the day of the enquiry the matron was stated to be 'indisposed' and her deposition took place in the master's sitting room. It was attended by Mr Cane, the Revd Hon. Mr Howard, Mr Turner and the clerk. She confirmed that she was in the habit of selling off milk only when she could spare it, not only to the Guardians but also but others not officially connected with the workhouse. Unfortunately it seemed that the master, Mr Turner, did not keep accounts of the amounts sold, but stated that he felt that they were no more than £1 in total. The porter stated that 'most persons in the town had been in the habit of sending to the workhouse for milk and cream and it had started in the time of the previous master, Mr Mitchell'.

The porter, a Mr Straw, was interviewed. He repeated that when Mr Mitchell was the master, many persons had been in the habit of buying milk and cream at the workhouse. The porter had to keep an account of all the visitors to the workhouse and the porter's book listed that on 22 May 1872, the clerk John Barrass's domestic servant called for milk and cream. The same servant had called the previous year on 18 November and 29 November and 11 and 20 December. The book also listed that 'Hinchcliffe's girl' went to the workhouse for milk, although the date is not mentioned. It seems that Mr Sharp was collecting evidence of mismanagement throughout the investigation as further developments were reported: not only was milk being sold off from the Rotherham workhouse, but also the tins of meat which had been bought for the inmate's consumption. Mr Sharp's evidence listed that on 5 December 1871, six cans of preserved meat were taken by a pauper called George Smith, aged fifteen, under instruction from the workhouse clerk. They were given to a man staying in the local inn. On the 14 December another further three cans were taken by the same boy; all this happened in the time of the present master, Mr Turner. Mr Barrass claimed the tins were a gratuity from the contractor J.W. Bellatt, of Thames Street, London. Mr Barrass's attention was swiftly brought to Article 218 of the Poor Law Regulations which forbid this practice and he assured the hearing that this would not happen again. At this point Mr Barrass became concerned that his name was being besmirched; the enquiry decided to go no further on this point, and the allegation was withdrawn.

In order to investigate the matter properly, Mr Cane asked that the porter's book listing visitors to the workhouse be sent for. However, when the book was brought into the enquiry it appeared that the relevant page was missing! Mr Straw stated that the matron, Mrs Turner, had requested that it be sent for about four or five minutes after a visit to the workhouse from Mr Sharp on the 2 July 1872; he added that he had given the book to Mrs Turner himself, who said that her husband was requesting it. Mrs Turner said that she had returned the book approximately four hours later and stated that she had not looked at it. The porter swore that the book was intact prior to this but when asked if he had reported the missing page to the Guardians, he replied that he hadn't. Without the relevant evidence it was agreed that the allegations regarding the milk would have to be withdrawn. What Mr Sharp thought about this is not recorded...

Mr Sharp then reverted back to his previous allegations of the large amounts of relief which had been distributed. Mr Cane stated that the Guardians maintain that the costs of relief had escalated for two reasons: one, 'a greater price given for provisions that is given in neighbouring towns and secondly the cost of the considerable outlay for the missing clothing which had to be replaced'. Mr Cane stated that he believed that the conduct of the late master (Mr Mitchell) in the matter of the paupers' clothing should have led to an enquiry, and the Guardians could only agree. The high cost of relief was answered by the chair to the Guardians, the Hon. Revd Mr Howard, who informed the enquiry that the year before there had been a 'great prevalence of fever and extra cost of rates was due to providing nurses and extras'. He said that there was overcrowding in the sick wards and pointed out to Mr Cane that on the 4 November he himself had written in the visitor's book: 'I am struck by the large proportion of sick, old and infirm in the workhouse. Out of a total of 154 [inmates] over half (84) are on the medical list, 22 receiving relief on account of old age. There are as many as 70 or 80 tramps accommodated per week'.

Mr Barrass was called, and he brought his bills with him. From these he deduced that the cost of in maintenance for the half year from 1868-1872 was 4s 4d per week per head. He also pointed out that from March last, there was a large increase in sickness in the Rotherham workhouse and during the half year ending Michaelmas 1871, the extras had increased. He went on, 'not only have the numbers of sick increased, but the treatment was more liberal'. Mr Cane also noted that the Rotherham Guardians gave out relief for non-resident poor and criticised it as being 'the most objectionable form of relief'. He was aware that the Guardians had no control over the persons giving the relief and no persons could vouch for that relief. Cane asked Mr Barrass if this was indeed so, and Mr Barrass affirmed that it was. He stated that he felt that £5 14s given each week for non-resident poor was correct and properly administrated. Mr Cane took pains to point out that relief of this kind should always be given in half and half.

Alderman John Guest indicated to the Guardians the great pains that the clerk, Mr Barrass, and the master, Mr Turner, had gone to obtain the information needed by Mr Cane. He admitted that the result was not satisfactory, however: it was difficult to compare the figures because 'the Rotherham Guardians offer a better dietary contract for best provisions including bread, prime beef and mutton and high priced wine and spirits'. (You will note there was no mention of 'old milk'.) Despite this statement, on examining the tenders for provisions recorded in the minutes, it seems that the Guardians inevitably awarded contracts to the lowest tenders for provisions; 'prime beef or mutton' were nowhere to be found in the list of provisions advertised in the local newspapers. Alderman Guest stated that the increased expenditure was also due to the increased numbers of sick paupers in the hospital, the cost of wines and spirits being £29 for spirits and £12 9s 1d in extras due to the number of inmates in the hospital in 1871 (which was sixty-five more than it had been in 1870). He stated that the Guardians had completed all their tasks as fairly as they possibly could, and that they believed:

> ...that destitute persons should be treated as human beings and their unhappy lot should not be unnecessarily embittered by harsh demeanour or that homes, however humble, should not be broken up when temporary relief only is required. Despite better diets, clothing etc it is satisfactory to the Guardians that it involves no levying of higher rates in the town.

On the next day the third complaint was investigated more fully. In the matter of the alterations from the plans it was stated that the workhouse building committee were often in attendance at the hospital and the fever wards and no deviation from the plans had been noted or reported by them. It seems probable that there had been some changes to the plans, though, as Mr Cane brought the Guardians' attention to Article 45 of the Poor Law Regulations where 'plans should not have been deviated from without the sanction of the Poor Law Board'. The Poor Law architect, Mr George Newsby Abbott, reported that he had visited the fever wards often and when they were completed on 21 December 1870 he compared the building with the plans and specifications and found:

> The excavations were not carried out according to the specifications plans.
> The building was higher than it should have been.
> The gateposts were not according to the plan.
> The palisade was much lighter than it should have been: instead of 5ft 3in, it was 2ft 9in.
> The spouting was only supported by wooden blocks instead of being made of stone.
> The flagging was of a more inferior type of stone than had been ordered.
> The rising of the stairs varied from three inches to eight inches.
> They had installed an iron sink instead of a stone one.

It was unclear from the enquiry as to whether any of these issues had been brought to the attention of the Guardians. However, Mr Newsby Abbott stated that the architect and surveyor for the workhouse, Mr Thomas Dobbs, had examined the final bill for the work completed on the workhouse and had found nothing wrong.

At this point the solicitor for Mr Sharp and the others stated that his clients had no apology for the issues surrounding the milk, and they had no intention of imputing any dishonesty on the part of anyone. He would leave the matter of the deviations from the building's plans in the hands of the Poor Law inspector, Mr Cane. However, he did feel that the charges regarding the comparative extravagance of the Guardians had been substantially supported. Mr Cane then brought the proceedings to an end. He agreed with Hon. Revd William Howard:

> That several important ratepayers of the union having misgivings as to the management of the workhouse and it was desirable that they have full information laid before them... which they might have been if they had applied to the Guardians... He was sure that the Guardians had given every possible facility for the gaining of information and he hoped the enquiry would lead to very great good in the union.

Mr Cane closed by saying that he was 'glad that the enquiry had begun and that he was also very glad that it had finished', to which comment there was some laughter. It is interesting to note that on the next board meeting for the Guardians that thanks were given to both Mr Guest and the Hon. Revd Mr Howard 'for the labour and trouble taken in the resulting charges brought against them and their officials by Mr Sharp and for the able manner in which they had conducted the case before the Poor Law Board'. They went further 'by deeply sympathising with Mr Barrass (clerk) and the master and matron for the very unpleasant position in which they have been placed by the charges brought by Mr Sharp'.

Whichever way you look at the enquiry, the charges brought against the Guardians did not reflect well on the officials or the Guardians themselves, and would perhaps indicate the way in which all workhouses were run – that the 'creaming off' of food and goods which were supposed to be consumed by the paupers themselves was a natural 'perk' of the job. It was confirmed in the enquiry that most people in the town were aware that the workhouse was acting as a dairy in selling milk and cream. The porter's book lists the Hon. Revd Mr Howard buying milk from the workhouse and the same book noted a Fanny Jobb also getting milk from the workhouse, so it seems that a large number of townspeople were aware of what was happening. Mr Edwards, the solicitor, made the point that other Guardians sent for milk, 'but was sure that they paid the required sum'.

Certainly in April 1872, just after the first enquiry with Mr Cane, the minutes note that 'no extras will be given by this board except on the responsibility of the relieving officers'. Nevertheless, the cost of wine and spirits remained high and in the fourth quarter of 1871 the cost of wine, brandy and gin supplied at Rotherham workhouse totalled £42 15s 6d. By comparison, in Wakefield during the same period the cost of supplying wine to the workhouse was only £4. It was also established at the same enquiry that no tenders were asked for alcohol; it was on the recommendation of one of the Guardians that the alcohol be bought from a 'respectable tradesmen of the town', a matter which could be open to abuse. Although no accusations could be made against any officer of the workhouse from this distance in time, the investigation indicated that accounts were not being kept accurately, some sharp practices had been uncovered and it is probable that some of this mismanagement had involved the Rotherham Guardians.

Embarrassingly for the Guardians, at the same time as investigations were being made by Mr Cane into the Guardians' mismanagement of the workhouse, a further allegation about the treatment a smallpox patient had received in the workhouse hospital was made by a patient, Mr William Shaw. The first the Guardians heard about the allegation was when a letter was received by the editor of the local newspaper, the *Rotherham Advertiser*, on 6 July 1872. Mr Shaw of 36 Burrell's Row, Westgate, had been brought into the smallpox hospital on 6 June at nine o'clock in the evening suffering from the disease. The Guardians had previously agreed with the Rotherham Corporation that in order to prevent contagion in the town, anyone suffering from smallpox could isolate themselves in the workhouse hospital's infectious wards (which had been cleared for the purpose). Mr Shaw was aware that he had contracted the disease and because he shared a house with his wife and another couple, and in order to prevent further infection, he went voluntarily to the hospital. He was met by Nurse East and she told two other patients, Arthur Crisp and Frank McGennis, to get out of their beds and go downstairs as one of the beds was needed for Mr Shaw. The patients (who had been undressed) then got out of the beds and put their clothes on. The nurse then instructed Mr Straw to get into one of the beds. He protested that the sheets had not been changed and noted that in fact he could see some of the crusts from the previous patient in the bed. Another patient, Thomas Garner, witnessed that Mr Shaw was asked to get into a dirty bed. He stated that prior to this incident a previous patient had occupied the same bed and the bedding had not been changed on that occasion either.

On 1 May 1848 the same allegations had been made at the Huddersfield workhouse and were widely reported in the national press. Patients had been instructed to get into beds which had been used several times by smallpox victims without the bedding being changed. It was also alleged that the hospital bedding had not been changed for periods of up to nine weeks. The scandal reverberated in the press, adding fuel to the debate of the atrocities suffered by workhouse inmates, yet twenty-four years later no lessons had been learned.

Mr Shaw also complained in his letter that the diet in the workhouse hospital was not sufficient for people who were ill. During his stay he had received 6oz of dry bread and a can of liquid supposed to be tea, but with no milk in it. Then for dinner there was rice pudding 'without milk or sauce' and the same as breakfast for supper. In addition to this to drink, they were given two cans of milk and water a day. He asked the editor, 'Is this a fit meal for a sick person?' He stated that when patients recover and are able to walk they go to the recovery ward, where they receive a can of 'skilley' and 6oz of dry bread for breakfast and supper. He alleged that some of the paupers in the workhouse get buttered bread and tobacco and two pints of beer a day. Yet the hospital patients were expected to drink water and smoke tea leaves and potato parings. Mr Shaw stated that to supplement his meal his wife had sent him 4ozs of butter on a green and white saucer, yet he only received 2ozs and no saucer. (Later on it was revealed that a workhouse 'washerwoman' was selling ¼lb (4oz) of butter for 1½d.) He ended his letter by stating that, 'This is not right in my eyes. The above account is true and I challenge the Guardians who think they can deny any of the above statements to insert their contradictions in next week's issue'. (*RAMA*, 6 July 1872)

He signed his name and gave his address and dated the letter 3 July 1872. The following board day the Guardians requested that the master ask Mr Shaw to appear before them in order to question him. Mr Shaw explained that he was a stranger to Rotherham and had been employed by Mr Favell of Westgate, Rotherham, for about sixteen or seventeen weeks. He was concerned about spreading the disease and had taken the advice of the many placards around the town asking for anyone who contracted smallpox to go straight to the workhouse hospital. At the close of the meeting, the press were admitted into the boardroom and the Guardians concluded that they had investigated the matter thoroughly and that the charges were entirely unfounded. They stated that the treatment for smallpox patients in the workhouse hospital was, on the whole, satisfactory. At a further meeting which the press attended on the 13 July 1872, Mr Shaw was described by the reporter as being a man with an imperfect education and his conduct before the Guardians contrasted favourably to the way in which 'he was received'. It was reported that when questioned, he did not fail to answer every charge made to him. Yet one of the Guardians – Alderman Guest himself, no less – accused him of 'exaggeration', 'ingratitude' and 'vituperation'. Another Guardian, Alderman Neil, protested against such wholesale denunciation of Mr Shaw and said that rather 'he deserves commendation' for bringing the matter to the Guardians' attention.

Mr Shaw was asked why he had not complained to one of the officers of the workhouse or a Guardian after being discharged from the hospital on the 20 June, and he said that he had intended to speak to the master but had not seen him. He was a stranger to the town and therefore didn't know any of the Guardians or where they lived (*RAMA,* 20 July 1872). There ensued a discussion about the 'skilley' (which was made of oatmeal). Mr Shaw said that it looked like milk, but he stated that it was not like milk and many of the patients would empty the meal out of the can and fill it with water to drink. The Guardians questioned the use of the term 'skilley', which was a term used in prison. Mr Shaw stated that he had never been in the House of Correction and that he heard the term being used by the ward man (*RAMA*, 13 July 1872). The Guardians were unable to agree and postponed the meeting until the following week of 20 July 1872.

The reporter stated that Mr Shaw's evidence was supported and supplemented by seven independent witnesses who were interviewed by the Guardians (who, concerned about collusion, ensured that all the witnesses who had left the room were unable to speak to each other). The reporter listed the people who gave evidence as Nurse Yarrold, an ex-assistant nurse, and two patients, Thomas Garner and Arthur Crisp, who vowed to the truth of Mr Shaw's statements regarding the food. The ward's man, Patrick Doyle, agreed that the patients preferred water to the skilley. Anne Yarrold, the nurse, stated that the skilley was not liked by the patients and described it as 'fearful stuff and not fit for a Christian'. It seems that the workhouse medical officer, Dr Hardwick, had ordered milk for him but he only had milk and water.

The complaints that his wife had sent him 4oz of butter and some oranges were 'proved conclusively'. When the washerwoman was questioned about selling the butter, she said that it had 'only been a lark'. The loss of food intended for the patients was not an isolated incident; one of the other patients, Arthur Crisp, stated that his mother had also sent into the hospital some tea, sugar and butter for him, none of which he received. Frank McGennis said that during his stay at the workhouse hospital he had been mistreated and on one occasion, being delirious, had got out of bed, which infuriated the ward's man Doyle, who threw him back onto the bed and threatened to 'throttle him'. Dr Hardwick agreed that people had complained about Doyle and that he had now been dismissed. Nurse Smith then appeared and was asked questions by the Guardians. She denied the bed was a dirty one and said that the bed was made up ready for him and clean sheets had been put on the bed. The reporter clearly stated that the evidence given by Shaw was consistent and supported by Dr Hardwick. He noted that Nurse Smith's statement was unsupported (*RAMA*, 20 July 1872).

Feelings about this complaint ran so high in Rotherham that the following week a public meeting was held at the Mechanics Hall on Effingham Street to investigate Mr Shaw's treatment and also the issues of the diet received by the paupers and the patients whilst in the workhouse. The reporters gleefully stated that the hall was crowded and the gallery was three parts occupied. He estimated that there were between 1,000 and 1,100 people in attendance. The chair, Mr R.H. Sharp (could this be the same Robert Henry Sharp who had called attention to the Guardians' alleged mismanagement?), started the proceeding by stating that he was aware that there was another case of mismanagement by the Guardians which was being investigated and asked that it 'not be alluded to'. The investigation was to concentrate just on the evidence in this case which was known as 'the smallpox case'. Mr Sharp said that anyone connected to the workhouse spoke very highly of the workhouse medical officer, Dr Hardwick, and his treatment of the patients. On entering the meeting room, Dr Hardwick addressed the Guardians and said, 'I am afraid this is a true case, gentlemen'. He confirmed that the case made by Shaw was, 'corroborative, consecutive, clear and unshaken and he could not see for the life of him how the Guardians could come to the decision they had, which no jury in England scarcely could have arrived at'.

Councillor Neil then got to his feet and was cheered as a hero when he began to speak. He said that he had pleasure in proposing a motion that 'it is in the opinion of this meeting the recent statements made by Mr Shaw and contained in a letter sent to the *Advertiser* were substantially confirmed and corroborated by the evidence adduced before the Rotherham Board of Guardians'. Mr John Weir seconded that resolution. The motion was then put to the meeting and the reporter noted that nearly every hand was held up to loud cheers. One of the enquiry, a Mr H.J. Wright, stated that he had no desire to say anything insulting about the Guardians, but felt that they were altogether unjustified in denouncing Mr Shaw's statements as 'vile and exaggerated'. Mr Wright went on to state that he 'proposed that this meeting is of the opinion that a Guardian committed a great indiscretion in condemning the statement of William Shaw as 'exaggerated' and 'vile' before hearing the facts, and the decision arrived at by the Guardians was against the weight of evidence brought before them.' (*RAMA*, 27 July 1872.)

Once again the Rotherham Guardians came out of the enquiry with no great dignity. Their hasty and summary dismissal of William Shaw's case indicates a desire not to bring attention to the ill treatment allegedly received by patients in the hospital. Unfortunately for them, the press got hold of the story, and it occupied the readers of the *Rotherham and Masbrough Advertiser* for three full weeks before culminating in a public enquiry that had been called by people wanting to know the truth. The Rotherham Guardians were keen to keep a lid on all of the allegations made against the practice of the workhouse and hospital officials and they were very lucky that, despite a public meeting, no further action was taken and no more publicity was given. Abuses such as these were relished by the national papers and the Rotherham Guardians were lucky that such a scandal was averted.

Circumstances of mysterious deaths were usually investigated by the Guardians or the Poor Law Board. This was true two years later when the death of John Batty, an inmate of Rotherham workhouse who had died at Wadsley under mysterious circumstances, was looked into. The attention of the case had been brought to the Guardians by Dr Clarke (the medical officer of Wentworth) and it was then reported in the local paper. In his letter to the Board of Guardians in January 1874, he apologised for troubling them but was concerned that on Monday 26 October 1873 he had examined William Batty at his home and he was found to be insane. He stated that, 'I escorted him to the Rotherham workhouse where I left him. The man was happy to go into the workhouse and to be left and there was no sign of any bodily injury'. Mr Batty was later admitted to Wadsley Asylum, where he died the following Thursday (30 October). On Saturday 1 November his widow went to the asylum after being told that he was dead and asked to see him, but this request was refused by the officials. His son and daughter requested to see his body on Monday 3 November, but they were also refused. The following day an inquest was held on his body following the post-mortem. It seems that Batty had died from inflammation of the lungs, accelerated by a broken rib. The asylum officials stated that the injury had not been caused at the asylum. No witnesses were called and no discussion was held as to how the injury had occurred. No further action had been taken for three months, until Dr Clarke grew concerned that the matter needed further investigation. He stated that he had thought of writing to the Commissioners for Lunacy, but he had wanted to place the matter before the Guardians to see if they felt that an investigation was needed. One of the Guardians asked if any enquiry had been made at Rotherham and it seems that several people had given evidence which had then been sent to Wadsley Asylum.

The Guardians agreed that the matter needed further investigation and sent the information to the West Riding justices. The clerk informed them that it would be laid before the visiting justices at their next meeting. It was agreed that Dr Clarke could write to the Commissioners for Lunacy, and he stated his intention to do so before the 26 January 1874 (*RAMA*, 27 January 1872). The Guardians championed his efforts and agreed that they 'see that nothing objectionable, rather the reverse of Dr Clarke's drawing it to the attention of the Commissioners'. The Guardians received a letter from the clerk to the visiting justices regarding the case and they found that the 'matter had been investigated by the coroner' and that 'no blame is imputed by the verdict to the officers of Rotherham union'. A letter from Dr Clarke was sent to the Guardians on the 23 February enclosing a letter from the Commissioners for Lunacy declining to enquire further into the matter.

The question of how Mr Batty gained his injuries and died is still unexplained. Lack of further evidence leaves us without answers. It was well known that pauper patents were cared for by other paupers (often those labelled as harmless lunatics or imbeciles) and the next case reveals yet more ill treatment of patients. Following this incident, the officials at Wadsley ensured that a certificate of health had to be written by the medical officer for the Rotherham workhouse before any patient would be admitted into the asylum. It certainly seems like there was some kind of cover up by the officials at Wadsley and/or at Rotherham.

The problems of under-staffing and using other inmates as carers were highlighted in a case of alleged flogging which was reported to the Guardians in September 1889 when it was brought to the attention of the board by one of the Guardians, Revd Blazeby. The information surrounding the case had been passed on to him by a ratepayer of the town. He reported that a pauper named William South, who was ill at the time (and had since died), was 'struck severely with a strap' by John Naylor, described as a ward man. Incredibly the strap was then given to an imbecile named John Page, who had also struck the man with the strap. The flogging had been witnessed by another inmate, William Dobson. It was reported in the local newspaper that the incident had occurred during the night and that South had died the next day. As the matter was so serious, members of the press were asked to leave the Guardian board room in order for the matter to be discussed 'in committee'. The press released information about it in the local newspaper, stating that 'so serious and damaging are the allegations that publicity ought to be given to the circumstances and as a consequence many ratepayers have manifested much indignation'. The newspaper concluded that 'the report of the committee to the board will be looked forward to with great interest' (*RAMA*, 5 October 1889).

A committee was ordered to investigate the matter and they reported back to the Guardians the following week. They agreed:

> That the employment of the strap by the imbecile John Page on the patient South is proved and is considered to be a most censorious proceedings. The handing of the strap by John Naylor who was put in to look after South to the said Page, constitutes a serious charge against the said Naylor.
>
> That John Naylor was seen by Benjamin Fligg who was making beds in the next ward to be present in the room while Page held the strap in his hand
>
> That with regard to the charge that John Naylor himself used the strap on South there is no evidence to prove this beyond the statement of Dobson. The fact that John Naylor absconded in workhouse clothing immediately an enquiry being made into his alleged flogging South is to be taken into account as substantiating that charge made by Dobson.

The committee do not see their way to form a judgement upon the charge against Joshua Naylor without further information.

A warrant was taken out for the arrest of John Naylor (aged seventy-four!) for absconding in workhouse clothing and he was arrested in Barnsley by Police Constable Bayliss. Mr Walton, the master, commented that Naylor was 'a very orderly man, he had never had any complaint made against him'. As a result of the absconding charge, he was committed to prison for fourteen days. It was stated by the committee that enquired into the alleged incident that they believed that 'there was not one witness brought before the committee that corroborated Dobson's story'. However, his statement when read out pointed to other witnesses being aware of the flogging. Mr Dobson stated that he had reported the matter to a Mr Charles Hague at the top of Westgate on Saturday 1 September. When asked why he had not reported it to the master, he said that he had heard of ill-usage before in the house and other people reporting such incidents to the master 'who took no notice of it' (*RAMA*, 19 October 1886). Apart from commenting that no useful purpose would be served in an official enquiry, no other comment was made by the Local Government Board. This is yet another incident where the Guardians do not come well out of the investigations, where matters are smoothed over in an attempt to rid themselves of all responsibility.

It seems that neglect of patients in workhouse hospitals was a common cause for complaint. A later scandal in Holborn workhouse involved a pauper named Timothy Daly, who died of neglect in St Bartholomew's Hospital. He had been taken by some of his friends out of the Holborn workhouse suffering from bedsores and extreme neglect. They at first sent him to private lodging, but his sufferings became so extreme that he was admitted to St Bartholomew's in December 1864, where he died the following day. The post-mortem revealed that he had died from exhaustion, bed sores and rheumatic fever, adding that Daly had received inadequate care from the Poor Law Authorities. (Geoffrey Rivett, Poor Law Infirmaries, http://www.nhshistory.net/poor_law_infirmaries.html)

So it is not surprising that the following year yet another ill treatment of a patient was reported, indicating once again that no lessons had been learned by the Rotherham authorities. The complaint about the treatment of patients in the workhouse hospital was first made by the wife of William Sharp when she appeared before the Guardians in February 1875. The matter was examined after the board meeting (which lasted over two hours). It appeared that William Sharp, formerly a point's man employed by the Midland Railway, now a lunatic, had been improperly treated in the Rotherham workhouse following his admittance on 27 December of the previous year. His wife complained that he was not seen by the medical officer Dr Hardwick for fifteen hours following his admittance. During his examination his wife was in attendance, and when Mrs Sharp suggested to Dr Hardwick that putting cold cloths on his head had soothed him previously, he told her in no uncertain terms that 'he would not be dictated to by her'.

Mrs Sharp made a further visit to the workhouse to take some clean clothes for his transfer to Wadsley Asylum on the 29 December. When she was admitted, the porter,

William Lenton, told her, 'We shall have a bonny row when we get to Wadsley Asylum about your master and about his face being hurt'. She didn't understand what he was talking about until she saw her husband's face, which she described as being black from bruising. After they took Mr Sharp away in a cab to Wadsley, she went into the lunatic ward at the Rotherham workhouse and saw blood on the floor, on his bed and on his clothes. The porter's wife, Mrs Elizabeth Lenton, said that her husband had gone into the workhouse lunatic ward that morning about 7 a.m. and had shouted to her, 'Make haste and get up for I don't know what's amiss, the place is like a butchers shop'. Dr Hardwick explained that Sharp had hit his head on the iron bedstead and that he may have been having violent fits. He was suffering from hallucinations. It seems that he was attended by two tramps that were sent into the lunatic ward to tend him as no one else was available. The dubiousness of this practise would inevitably lead to accusations such as this.

A former friend of her husband's, a Mr Barnes of 18 Henry Street, Rotherham, then suggested she enquire at Wadsley Asylum 'about his broken ribs'. She went to Wadsley and saw the medical officer, Mr Mitchell, and asked him about her husband's broken ribs. Dr Mitchell asked how she knew about his ribs and then turned away and ignored her. The chairman of the Guardians spoke to a Justice who had seen Sharp before he went to Wadsley and was informed that he 'was never in the presence of a more violent lunatic'. It appears that when he arrived at Wadsley, the porter was asked to sign a book to the effect that the patient had broken ribs. Dr Hardwick stated that the porter was not qualified to judge whether a patient had broken ribs or not. He produced a letter from Dr Mitchell dated two or three days after Sharp's admittance and stating that he was unsure about whether Mr Sharp was suffering from broken ribs when admitted. When this was reported to the Poor Law inspector, Mr Cane, he suggested that a book be kept at the workhouse showing the condition of every lunatic on admission or discharge and that once again, prior to any patient being sent from the union to the asylum, a medical certificate be given to the medical officer at the asylum as to the patient's condition.

However, the officials of the workhouse were not reprimanded for this incident and it is perhaps a reflection on how lunatics were viewed by society. For whatever reason no further comments about Mr Sharp's injuries were made.

In March 1886 criticisms of one of the workhouse officials and the Guardians' actions themselves were made by two members of the Board of Guardians, Mr Benjamin Soresby and Mr William Badger. The minute book is missing so we have to rely on the newspaper reports of the time (with their inevitable sensational slant). It seems the two gentlemen had visited the workhouse as part of their duties as members of the visiting committee and had made comments in the visitor's book in February regarding the poor condition of the children in the workhouse. When they attempted to bring the matter to the Guardians' attention at the next board meeting the chair, Mr Jubb, refused to look into the matter and attempted to move onto the next business. Messrs Soresby and Badger were incensed by this and they sent a report to the Local Government Board asking them to look into the matter. They issued a statement which the clerk was obliged to read out at the board meeting stating the allegations were that:

> The matron was not fulfilling her duties to visit the wards daily and to take general supervision of the women inmates as per the Consolidated Order page 206 Article 210 paragraph 5 & 6.
>
> That a suitable caretaker be appointed for the children
>
> There had been ill-treatment of an imbecile pauper by an officer of the workhouse.

The Local Government Board passed the complaints to the Board of Guardians and asked for their comments. All matters which had been reported in the visitor's book had to be investigated by the Guardians, so it is difficult from this point in time to understand the reluctance of the chair to look into these matters or his attempt to dismiss them out of hand. The only suggestion could be that these two Guardians appear to be amongst the most contentious during the meetings and were often outspoken in their dealings, as reported in the minutes. In the report, Messrs Soresby and Badger first claimed that when visiting the aged women's ward they had received a complaint that the matron, Mrs Walton, 'only visits the wards once a week in some wards and once a fortnight in others'. According to the Consolidated Order, it was part of the matron's duties that she was expected to visit the wards on a daily basis to ensure that the patients were properly cared for and to listen to any complaints. Messr Badger and Soresby then complained about the state of the children, claiming that no caretaker was employed to look after the children and as a consequence, the visiting committee found young children 'dirty and slovenly'. They also reported that they found children in the same room of the infectious hospital, where adults were suffering from syphilis. This they thought to be morally unacceptable. Messrs Badger and Soresby had also investigated a complaint by an imbecile pauper who claimed that the porter had kicked him. These two Guardians reported to the other members of the board that they had inspected the body of the unfortunate lunatic, who 'showed evidence of his ill-usage by the porter'.

Curiously the chairman tried to stop the clerk from reading the allegation out to the other Guardians, but the clerk reminded him that he was bound to read it as it came from the Local Government Board. The chair complained that these matters had been before the Guardians and had been dealt with, and no other complaint had been heard from any other member of the visiting committee. Mr Jubb asked the clerk to reply to the Local Government Board stating that the matter enquired of by Messrs Badger and Soresby had been looked into and the opinion of this Board of Guardians was that the condition of the house was satisfactory. He requested that a report be sent, with a medical report, from the medical officer as to the alleged injury to the imbecile.

There appeared to be no further enquiry into the allegations of the matron or the state of the workhouse children, but Mr Walton, the workhouse master, was then called and asked whether the inmate referred to had been kicked by the porter. The master stated that there was no truth in the allegations. It was resolved that at this point the matter was dismissed, the only dissenting voice being that of Mr Soresby (*RAMA*, 20 March 1886). This did not satisfy Messrs Badger and Soresby; they wrote a letter to the editor of the *Rotherham Advertiser* appealing for the chance to be heard. The letter was published on the 13 March. In the letter they stated that:

> Some Guardians visit the workhouse and sign the book without visiting the inmates who have said 'we seldom see the other Guardians but you'. The Consolidated Order states that the workhouse should be visited at least once a week and to examine carefully the workhouse in every detail and afford to the inmates every opportunity to complain regarding food, clothing and treatment and then sign the book. We visited on Saturday… and asked the master for a copy of the Consolidated Orders but he could not supply it.

Nothing further about this matter was recorded in the local newspaper, but these two Guardians continued to challenge their colleagues and their names occur many time throughout the minutes.

In November 1890, a letter arrived from the Local Government Board asking for an investigation to be made into allegations about the master, Mr Walton, who, it was claimed, had seriously neglected his duties and that he had kept to himself the fact that two bastard children had been born in the workhouse. He had not reported this matter to the Board of Guardians. An investigation was held and it was concluded that 'the Guardians consider that Mr Walton had shown himself unfit for his post'. They therefore required him to place his resignation in the hands of the Guardians. The problem started when it had been decided, in 1885, that as the children were now attending the Wellgate Board School in the town, there was no need to employ a schoolmaster or a schoolmistress. Instead, a caretaker for the children was to be appointed. A Miss Thornton was elected to the post and when she tendered her resignation in August 1885 it was agreed that a sub-committee look into the six applicants for the post on the 5 October. However, probably in an attempt to save money, the committee disregarded the six applicants and advised that a pauper inmate with four children take over the duties of caretaker as she 'constantly helped the previous caretaker in her duties'.

The name of this proposed caretaker was a Miss Priscilla Smith, aged thirty-eight, from Dudley in Staffordshire. The Guardians approved the decision and resolved that she take over the duties for the time being and requested that the arrangement was supervised by the matron. One of the illegitimate children whose existence the master had concealed had belonged to Priscilla Smith – and an allegation had been made that the child was his. The Guardians investigated the allegations and stated – that as regards the paternity of Priscilla Smith's child – the evidence showed that she was a woman with 'no regard for truth and that her statements on oath are contradicted by her own statements at other times'. The Guardians continued that 'her testimony has not been corroborated in any material particular and the Guardians consider that she has entirely failed to establish her allegation that the master is the father of her child'.

A report was completed to be sent to the Local Government Board when more revelations about the conduct of Priscilla Smith were made. It was established that:

> Priscilla Smith, a woman of notoriously loose character, was granted five days leave of absence and allowed to leave her children behind her in the house. Nothing could be more dangerous or irregular than to allow the mother of bastard children to leave their offspring in charge of the workhouse authorities. Such women may disappear or as it seems happened in Smith's case may return again pregnant to throw a further burden on the rates.
>
> It appears that Priscilla Smith has for some time past and by the direction of the Guardians been discharging duties in the workhouse usually allowed to an officer and by way of compensation has been allowed a number two diet and a gill of beer daily. An able bodied pauper with her antecedents should never be placed in such a position of authority and responsibility. Smith has abused her privileges by giving birth to another illegitimate child and if she is still getting the extra allowance above mentioned, these should be forthwith discontinued.
>
> It appears that Smith when temporarily out on leave was allowed to go abroad wearing her own clothes. It is doubtful whether the able bodied mother of bastard children ought to have any leave at all but at any rate the practice of allowing paupers to go out in their own clothes is one that cannot be approved.

It seems that part of the blame was laid at the matron's door for lack of supervision of Smith as the Guardians ordered that another caretaker be appointed as soon as possible. They also demanded an additional female officer – an assistant matron, a laundress or a cook – to 'thus set free the matron to enable her to exercise that larger amount of general supervision which seemed to be urgently required'. The master, Mr Walton, was instructed to resign immediately. However, Miss Smith was unable to leave the workhouse and was still a resident in the Rotherham workhouse in the census of 1891. (1891 Census Rotherham Union Workhouse, www.rotherhamweb.co.uk/h/twhous.htm) What they failed to investigate, however, was the fact that she had been chosen over six other genuine applications (which may have saved the Guardians some embarrassment over the way that workhouse staff had been elected).

An investigation into the case of the other illegitimate child, the knowledge of whose birth had been withheld by the master from the Guardians, was looked into the following month in December 1890. Due to its delicate nature the matter was dealt with as swiftly as possible. The first the Guardians heard was when the master alleged that a female inmate of the house had been outraged (raped) by Dr Hardwick's assistant, Dr Jones. It was stated that she had 'connections' with him on two separate occasions. Statements had been taken from the portress, from Nurses Downing and Walker as well as from the master and matron (and of course from the pauper herself, Miss Lavinia Hoyland). Doctors Hardwick and Jones appeared before the Guardians (who naturally chose to investigate the delicate matter 'in committee'). Dr Hardwick stated that when he employed Dr Jones, he was given good references. Dr Jones then appeared and flatly denied the allegations, saying they had no foundation whatsoever. He declared that he was prepared to deny under oath the charge made against him. It was agreed that a special board meeting would be held on 22 December 1890, to which Lavinia Hoyland was to be summoned. Although the press were excluded from the enquiry, it appears that this was not the first time such an allegation had been made. In the *Rotherham and Masbrough Advertiser* for 27 January 1877, thirteen years previously, a similar accusation was made that:

> …a week or two ago some serious allegations were made from a pauper female patient against an assistant of one of the medical officers. Of course the Guardians have to investigate. They did so behind closed doors and reporters were denied entrance. After the meeting the Guardians unanimously passed a severe resolution condemning the party who brought the charge.

In the case of Lavinia Hoyland it was agreed that a special board meeting would be held for the Guardians to review all the evidence. It was a very lengthy hearing and at its conclusion it was agreed that all the evidence be forwarded to Mr Kennedy, the Poor Law inspector. Shortly after this meeting the visiting committee had considered the need for more supervision in the house and the need for more staff to be appointed. The only further reference was a report that the clerk had informed the board that Mr Kennedy had been to see him and had stated that: 'in the case of Lavinia Hoyland he should do nothing unless the Guardians decide to take the initiative of reporting the case'.

No further mention is made of the case, but 'Lavinia Hoyland' is listed in the 1881 census at the age of nineteen. Ten years later, in the 1891 census referenced above, she is listed as a thirty-year-old domestic servant from Handsworth, Sheffield. She originated from Fence, Yorkshire, and she was still living there in 1901, aged thirty-nine, having spent twenty years in the workhouse at Rotherham, though by now she is listed on the census as a charwoman from Sheffield. (See the 1901 Census, RMBC Rotherham Archives and Local Studies Department.)

The complaints about mismanagement of the Rotherham Board of Guardians and the allegations brought against them appear to have some level of accuracy. However, due to the distance of time it is hard to judge with any authority. The Guardians do not seem to investigate any of the issues as thoroughly as they should and the conclusions they arrive at are often questionable – but perhaps lessons were learned. Certainly from the 1890s, it seems that other deaths of pauper inmates were noted in the minutes but not elaborated on. Perhaps the Guardians were becoming more adept at concealing details from the local press?

For example, in January 1895 it was minuted that Dr Robinson, the workhouse medical officer, had reported to the Poor Law Board the sudden deaths (on the 11 and 14 January) of two inmates, Catherine Haley and Michael O'Brian. The Local Government Board requested that a report on the inquests of the two paupers to be sent to them, but nothing further is recorded. Quite unusually, there is nothing about the two deaths in the local newspapers, even though previously they had been very adept at ferreting out more details. Further particulars were requested from the Guardians later that year, in August 1895, regarding the sudden death of one Olive Abdellah, who died from 'being accidentally burnt'. A report of the inquest and full particulars were sent to the Local Government Board, but once again there is no report in the local press.

Whilst I don't think the Guardians intentionally tried to conceal any serious crimes, I do feel that their experience at the hands of the local newspapers had taught them some lessons and serious matters were investigated in a more closed and private manner then previously. Investigative measures involved a lot of paperwork and time, and therefore any unreported abuse would have left many inmates of the workhouse in a very vulnerable position. The low pay of the officers of the workhouse usually attracted the lower sort of person who more often that not might take out their frustrations on the inmates. Cases which were investigated where no blame was laid by the Guardians at the feet of the officers would only ensure a regime of brutality for the pauper inmates. The Andover scandal (where paupers were reduced to sucking the gristle off the bones intended for breaking) revealed that the master and matron committed abuses such as flogging, sexual abuse and stealing the inmates' food. Yet following the outcry, after their actions became public knowledge and their resignation was accepted, no further action was taken against the master, and he went on to take up another post at another workhouse.

Having closely examined the Guardians' minutes, it has to be said that at Rotherham the Guardians worked very closely with the Poor Law Board and, despite some accusations, endeavoured to provide the best for their inmates. This is indicated by the many kind acts of the Guardians (i.e. the paupers sent to Buxton Baths for recuperative purposes, or the inmates allowed time out of the workhouse regardless of the Consolidated Orders). Nonetheless, many of the criticisms aimed at the Rotherham Guardians were justified. During the period of study, more and more national scandals were reported in the newspapers of the time and the Guardians of the Rotherham workhouse were lucky that they did not receive the same publicity and outcry as many of the other reported cases.

And so I come to the end of my study of the Rotherham workhouse. Fortunately today there is no need for such organisations, and the welfare state ensures that people do not starve to death. The overall impression I get regarding the Guardians of the Rotherham workhouse is, that despite coming from a different strata of society, they really did try to afford relief for the poor people of the town at a time when the prevailing attitude was that workhouse paupers brought their condition on themselves by their own idleness. History, and I hope this book, indicates that this was just not true. The softening of the attitude of the Guardians and the people of the town of Rotherham are seen in the many treats afforded the pauper inmates. Workhouse inmates were generally families and individuals who were the most powerless victims of the dictates of the Poor Law Board and the commands of the Guardians of the Poor.

Appendix

Some of the Workhouse Paupers Mentioned in the Guardians' Minutes

These are just some of the paupers that are mentioned in the minutes. This is by no means a comprehensive list.

21.8.37 Richard Guest to receive relief of 2s 6d weekly. Widow Woodhead for a loan of £4 10s for the purchase of a mangle and that weekly relief to her be discontinued.

4.9.37 William Reynolds paid to the relieving officers for his funeral: 2s 6d plus 13s for his coffin. Elizabeth Johnson of Aston paid 6d a week extra in consideration of the trouble occasioned by relieving officers paying the poor at her cottage. The son of Widow Roebuck of Rawmarsh be proceeded against for the support of his mother.

11.9.37 Coffin and funeral expenses for Mary Kesteven £1 2s 11d. Coffin and funeral expenses for George Apsley, £1 2s. That the medical officers report on the case of Josh Robinson, a bastard child. That the overseers of Maltby proceed against John Richards, the husband of Mary Richards, for the maintenance of his wife. That Elizabeth Gillam, a lunatic, the wife of George Gillam of Treeton, be sent to Wakefield Asylum, and that the husband pay 1s a week towards the expense.

18.9.37 The overseers of Scarborough be paid the sum of £1 2s 6d for the board of Sarah Mallinson, a pauper belonging to Rotherham Parish and the further sum of £1 1s for the expense of removing her from Scarborough to the West Yorkshire pauper Lunatic Asylum, she being a lunatic.

25.9.37 The matron of Rotherham workhouse produced an account due to Michael Steer for the funeral amounting, with church fees, to 8s 6d. An application be made to the court of the quarter sessions for an order upon George Wright for the maintenance of an bastard child on the body of Ann Wade.

9.10.37 The services of the nurse attending Rebecca Oldham be continued as a salary of 7s a week until further notice. That William Parker be allowed 3s for relief for this last week. See his son John to enquire if he will do anything towards his support.

16.10.37 The overseers of Rotherham be authorised to apply to John Burgan for maintenance of an bastard child.

23.10.37 The relieving officer to furnish Mary Heelaw of Brampton with wine and other necessities as recommended by the medical officer for a week.

6.11.37 The clothes supplied to Anne Spencer whilst in the workhouse be considered a loan and that her first half year's wages after leaving the workhouse be attached for repayment of the loan. A cheque for £2 1s 6d be given to Benjamin Brown for the expense of getting the body of James Strafford, a pauper of Kimberworth, out of the water.

13.11.37 The relieving officer pay to Joseph Thompson 2s, he being a casual pauper.

20.11.37 A week's relief amounting to 10s be advanced to Benjamin Woodhouse of Brinsworth to enable him to get out of debtors' jail at Sheffield.

18.12.37 That 1s a week be received out of the wages of Thomas Copley towards repayment of expenses incurred in maintenance of his family in the workhouse.

1.1.38 An order of maintenance be obtained against – Newton for a child born on the body of Avril Hoyland of Swinton. An order against ---- ---- for a child on the body of Sarah Sykes of Swinton. That two changes of clothes be provided for Elizabeth Brown of Maltby if Thomas Shearer will take her as an apprentice.

8.1.38 An order of maintenance be obtained against the father of an bastard child born on the body of Hannah Denton of Swinton.

15.1.38 An order of maintenance be obtained against William Pew for the maintenance of a bastard child born on the body of Ann Watson of Rotherham.

22.1.38 The wages of William Wilkinson of Masbrough (moulder) be attached for the maintenance of his wife Sarah Wilkinson ordered into the workhouse.

29.1.38 20s be paid to Elizabeth Brown of Maltby to provide with suitable clothes on her going into the service of Thomas Shearer of Sheffield. Coffin for Anne Burgun of Greasbrough.

5.2.38 That Peter Day of Wentworth be advanced a loan of 2s worth of bread per week until his health is restored.

19.2.38 That the wages of Joshua Best working at Messrs Taylors at Rawmarsh be attached for the maintenance of his mother.

26.2.38 That Henry Fleming of Rotherham be proceeded against as the law directs for not maintaining his wife and family.

12.3.38 That William Wright of Rawmarsh be summoned before the magistrate for the maintenance of his wife.

26.3.38 Thomas Parker near St George's church, Sheffield be summoned for the maintenance of his father William Parker belonging to Rotherham.

4.6.38 John Richardson of Rotherham be bound by Parish Indentures to William Rawson of Sheffield and that £1 5s be paid to his master for clothes.

25.6.38 That Thomas Penthorpe of Aston be sent to Wakefield House of Correction for the neglect of his family.

2.7.38 The assistant overseer of Rotherham reported that he had, pursuant to directions of the Guardians, summoned Charles Whiteley before the magistrates at Sheffield who had committed him to the Wakefield House of Correction for six weeks in neglecting his family. The assistant overseer of Rotherham reported that he had summoned Thomas Penthorpe before the Magistrates in Rotherham who had committed him to Wakefield House of Correction for one month. An order against John Hattersley for a maintenance order of a female bastard child of Mary Longthorne.

20.8.38 Order that John Cousins of Wickersley be sent to Buxton for the benefit of his health.

7.1.39 That Charles ---- be summoned before the magistrate to show cause why he doesn't maintain his mother; that William Muscroft be summoned before the magistrate to show just cause why he does not maintain his wife and family.

22.7.39 That a warrant be taken out against Louisa Clark of Rotherham and Mary Brown of Maltby for running away out of the workhouse.

2.9.39 Thomas Copley of Brampton Bierlow having been apprehended by warrant for again neglecting his children and refusing to maintain them. Ordered that an application be made to the justices to commit him to Wakefield House of Correction until the Sheffield Sessions and then be dealt with according to law. Assistant overseer of Brampton Bierlow be allowed to charge the sum of 12s to the constable of Chapeltown for apprehending Thomas Copley for neglect of his family. Ordered that Francis Barwick be summoned before the magistrate for the maintenance of his mother and father at Wentworth.

21.10.39 Ordered that Francis Barwick be summoned before the magistrates for the maintenance of his father and mother at Wentworth.

18.11.39 The assistant overseer of Wentworth be allowed to pay William Pepper, constable, the sum of 9d for serving a summons on Francis Barwick for the support of his parents.

11.5.40 That an advertisement be inserted in the *Doncaster Gazette* and Sheffield newspaper for the apprehension of William Arundell who has absconded, leaving his wife and family chargeable to the parish of Rotherham, and that a reward of £2 be offered for his apprehension.

18.5.40 Ordered that 10s be given to Ellen Connelly for giving information that led to the apprehension of Margaret Hogan, the mother of the child found at Brinsworth.

19.10.40 In the case of the man named John Sylvester having been taken from the Red Bear in Rotherham to the union workhouse in a supposed fit of apoplexy whereas it subsequently appeared that he was in a state of extreme drunkenness.

13.12.41 Cheque for £1 5s 9d be given to George Marshall his expenses and loss of time for journey to Derby after William Gillett, a pauper who had run away from the workhouse.

2.4.42 Read from the master's minute book about the misconduct of Ann Bamforth and John Cookson and the conduct of some of the able-bodied women is so bad a committee is formed to meet at the workhouse on Thursday next to ascertain whether the increased accommodation to admit a better classification of able-bodied females.

21.5.49 Read in the master's journal report on the conduct of Charles Turner's wife when it appeared to the board that there was no way to prevent it. They ordered that the wife should eat her meals in the dining hall along with the other inmates.

1.9.51 That the Poor Law Board be approached to sanction loan of £6 10s or less in order for Elizabeth Hodgson to proceed to America to join her daughter. Letter from the Poor Law Board refusing to sanction the proposed advance to Mrs Hodgson to go to America. An application be made to the board by Mrs Earnshaw, whose husband is in the pauper lunatic asylum chargeable to Treeton, for his discharge. Letters produced from the asylum stating that Earnshaw might be safely discharged with care. Ordered that the board refer to Dr Corsellus and that the board will sanction it if it could be done safely. That the Poor Law Board be requested to sanction the allowance of £5 for an operation by Mr Le Tall on Charles Gleadhill of Beighton. The operation being similar to that of a strangulated hernia. That the clerk write to the York union in response to an alleged case of improper treatment of Jane Austin by a beerhouse keeper in York.

17.5.52 Letter from Sheffield union *re* Frederick Gauty, a tramp. That he was refused relief at Rotherham. Statements from Mr Barrass, T Dearnally (porter) were read and a copy sent to the Poor Law Board saying that this board frequently receives complaints from Sheffield union clerk.

14.6.52 Read letter from the Poor Law Board with statements from Ann Whitely from Sheffield. Resolved unanimously that the answer should be as follows: 'The Rotherham Board of Guardians admit that they were paying Isaac Whitely through the hands of a relative from Masbrough up to his death. There have been similar cases where Rotherham paid out for Sheffield union. The Board of Guardians were informed by an Assistant Poor Law Commissioners that this practise was inconvenient and objectionable, but not illegal and that the Board of Guardians have often had occasion to express their deep regret at the refusal to pay poor people belonging to this union resident in the Sheffield union. The Board of Guardians state that the Sheffield union is the only one in England that they do not work harmoniously with and would welcome any investigation into any case between selves and the Sheffield union.'

3.1.53 Read letter from police superintendent at Howden announcing capture of two boys named Chester and McGee who absconded from the workhouse with workhouse dress. Ordered that he deliver the boys into the custody of Rotherham police.

6.6.53 Resolved that a recommendation be given to Thomas Robinson of Bramley chargeable to the establishment to Buxton Bath Charity, and 20s be allowed for travelling expenses.

13.6.53 Resolved that a recommendation be made to Buxton Bath Charity with 20s for expenses be given to George Malthouse chargeable to the establishment resident in Kimberworth.

1.8.53 Resolved that James England be applied to for the union clothing and if he refuses to be summoned.

24.4.54 Resolved that the medical officer be asked for information on the death of George Standway.

12.6.54 Resolved that the following inmates of the workhouse be allowed leave of absence: Elizabeth Robinson for two days and one night; Ann Mortimer for one week.

26.6.54 The master advised that two boys, John Chester and William Holland, had absconded from the union workhouse during the temporary absence of the schoolmaster. Resolved during the absence of the schoolmaster an official person be left in charge of the children to overlook them.

30.7.54 That John Froggatt of Maltby be allowed one week's absence from the workhouse and James Jarvis from Rawmarsh three days.

7.8.54 Resolved that ---- Goucher, a pauper, be allowed a week's leave of absence to see her friends.

14.8.54 The clerk reported that the son of William Simonite of Whiston residing at Sheffield proposed to pay 1s 6d per week towards his mother's maintenance by monthly instalments. Agreed.

12.2.53 Resolved that the mother of George Satterfill, who died in the workhouse last week, be allowed to have her son's clothes.

15.2.64 On the application of the father of Mary Ann Bennett that for the present she be retained in the workhouse the father undertaking to pay the cost of her maintenance after the rate of 7s per week from 25 January last.

25.7.64 That the Poor Law Board opinion be obtained on the power of the Guardians to incur any costs in assisting Mr Westerman, a pauper, to bring an action against the Midland Railway Co. for an accident damaging his foot.

1.8.64 Poor Law Board say Guardians have no power to bring action against Midland Railway Co.

20.2.65 Read letter from Messrs March and Edwards on subject of maintenance of Mr Wheeler's daughter, a lunatic in the asylum, offering to pay 2s a week towards her maintenance. Resolved he be required to pay 5s a week.

3.4.65 13s 6d each awarded to the police for apprehending Michael Fox and McAlpine.

22.5.65 The visitors' book was laid before the board containing the following observations of the woman Greaves who complains 'the nurse abuses her wherever she goes to wash the old women'. Mrs Bates (matron) has to go with her to protect her. Elizabeth Hudson also complains and a communication from Dr Hardwick was read on the subject of a supposed neglect of Smith's child in the hospital.

3.9.66 The chairman and clerk signed the usual certificate of Joseph Wragg, a lunatic, to enable his pension to be attached.

21.10.67 Mrs Ellison of Morthern be requested to attend the board to make some arrangement as to contributing towards her daughter's maintenance in the asylum.

24.8.68 In obedience of a request from Dr Hardwick, the medical officer, that he had visited Joseph Green and could not give benefit to his knee without amputation. He had even given him an expensive diet, but to no avail.

8.2.69 Request the medical officer to examine Henry Firkin, an imbecile now in the workhouse, and to make a special report.

15.2.69 Dr Hardwick reported that Henry Firkin is an unfit person to remain in the workhouse and is to go to an asylum.

15.3.69 Letter from the Poor Law Board regarding a report from the Commissioner for Lunacy regarding Hannah Hargreaves, residing at Wath, and inviting the Guardians' observations on it. Resolved that she had better be removed to the asylum.

2.8.69 Letter from the Poor Law Board regarding Peter Williams, a poor German boy now in the workhouse, referring to the Guardians to the Consulate General for the North of Germany, to whom the clerk reported he had applied.

22.11.69 Letter from the Consulate General (London) unable to discover any clue to the German boy.

28.1.70 Resolved that Dr Foote be requested to explain the circumstances under which he declined to attend Harriet Rhodes's child.

20.6.70 Resolved that the several poor persons whose names are hereunder written residing in the Rotherham union and being desirous of emigrating to Pittsburgh, America, the necessary steps to be immediately taken to effect the immigration and that a sum not exceeding £5 be expended for such persons to be charged upon the common fund of the union: Rachel Bethel, thirty years, widow; David Thomas Bethel, six years, her child; Albert Bethel, five years, her child.

27.6.70 Letter from the Poor Law Board in answer to the application on behalf of Rachel Bethel informing the Guardians that in consequence of the representations made by the Government of the United States they are unable to sanction emigration to that country at the cost of the poor rate.

13.11.71 Sarah Bates of Beighton took an orphan Sarah Bills, aged nine years, as recommended by the Boarding Out Committee of Beighton.

5.2.72 Thomas Gilroy of Swinton appeared before the Guardians and arranged to give authority to his employer Mr Blunn to pay to the union 8s a week towards the maintenance of his wife now in the asylum.

13.5.72 Letter from Mr Shaw who was called upon to maintain his grandchildren now in the workhouse. Resolved that the children be placed in the workhouse for one month to give Mr Shaw time to prepare for them.

17.2.73 Councillor Bray and the town missionary appeared before the Guardians to request that an orphan named Sarah Ryley should be removed from Mr Poulter's hotel, The Falstaff Inn, to Mullers Orphan Institution at Bristol. Resolved the Guardians do not interfere, the girl having expressed a desire to remain.

14.4.73 Letter from Mrs Armitage offering to keep Mary Ann Alford in the 'Home connected with the Wakefield House of Correction' if the Guardians would keep her child in the workhouse to give her 'an opportunity to be reformed'. Resolved that Mrs Armitage's offer be thankfully accepted.

3.11.73 The master reported that he had found £38 14s 3d on the body of the pauper Thomas Oldfield. Resolved that such money to be paid to the treasurer to the credit of this union.

8.12.73 Letter received from the Local Government Board *re* the property of Thomas Oldfield, deceased. Resolved that the clerk to take his instructions as to its disposal from the Board of Guardians.

10.8.74 Letter received from Leeds union informing the Guardians that they intend to bind out William Nolan, aged fourteen and now resident in Leeds workhouse, to Mr Isaac Charlton, blacksmith, of Wentworth, and requesting if the Guardians have any objection to be offered.

9.11.74 Edward Kingston of Wentworth is requested to pay 2s 6d a week for maintenance of his wife in the asylum.

24.1.76 Read letter from Mrs Doncaster complaining of the condition of two children called Richardson who had been sent from the workhouse to homes in Sheffield.

7.2.76 Letter from Mr Marsden informing the Guardians that Mary Ann Bennett had been sent to the West Riding Asylum by the justices and enquiring if the Guardians would admit her settlement and repay the cost of her maintenance without putting the county to the expense of taking out orders. Agreed.

14.2.76 Letter from Mr Marsden informing the Guardians that Ann Knapton had been sent to the West Riding Asylum by the justices and enquiring if the Guardians would admit her settlement and repay the cost of her maintenance without putting the county to the expense of taking out orders. Agreed.

13.3.76 Letter from Mr Marsden informing the Guardians that Daniel McIver Barton was taken to the West Riding Asylum.

27.11.76 The visiting committee report that a lunatic called Bloomfield was now resident in the workhouse although he desired to return home. His wife stated that she was not able to receive him at home but as Dr Mitchell felt he should be discharged, that he be sent home and relief given to him for one month on trial as recommended by Dr Hardwick.

29.1.77 Received letter from the Local Government Board *re* Elizabeth Tissington or Roberts who had been removed from the workhouse to the asylum at Wadsley.

That the bastard child not being chargeable, the putative father is not liable. Letter from George Wilton Chambers Esq enclosing letter from Mr Diggins, secretary of the Albert Asylum for Idiots, relative to the case of Henry Earnshaw, an imbecile in that institution.

11.6.77 Letter from Dr Mitchell (medical superintendent of South Yorkshire Asylum) stating that the warrant of the Secretary of State would be sufficient authority for him receiving the criminal lunatics Wood and Whittington.

10.9.77 Letter from Dr Walker, medical officer for Kimberworth, requesting extra medical fees of £2 2s for attending the case of Richard Lloyd daily and using the catheter (Richard having suffered from an enlarged prostate and paralysis of the bladder).

10.12.77 Letter from Dr Mitchell on the subject of the supposed loss of money from the person of Harriet Knowles who was sent from this union and is now an inmate. He promised to make strict enquiries into the matter and get the assistance of the police.

3.1.81 Clerk reported Hannah Dunmore, admitted to Wadsley Asylum on 21 June last, had died on 31.12.80.

10.1.81 Mr Adams attended the board to explain that his brother (who with his family had been in receipt of relief) had left a sum of money in the Post Office Savings Bank as a legacy from his father. It was resolved that his offer to pay £10 to the Guardians be accepted and that he be allowed to keep the remainder.

31.1.81 S.E. Sellars, removed to Wadsley, and William Bagnall, admitted on 29.4.80, had died on 21.1.81.

28.2.81 Clerk reported that Sarah Ann Barker had been removed by her friends from Wadsley Asylum.

14.3.81 Pheobe Lyalls of Rawmarsh had died at Wadsley.

21.3.81 Harriett Cavill removed from Wadsley by friends.

23.5.81 Enquiries to be made into the settlement of Bassendale admitted to the workhouse this day.

30.5.81 Clerk reported Elizabeth Robinson, pauper lunatic, admitted to Wadsley 18.2.80 and removed to Rotherham workhouse.

24.10.81 Order for Mr Dawson to pay 2s 6d towards the maintenance of his wife be rescinded, a letter being read proving his total inability.

31.2.82 Resolved that John Hyde be removed to the asylum at Wadsley from York Asylum where he was a private patient, Nicholson and Co. promising to pay the Guardians the amounts remaining in their hands of accounts of the estate.

27.3.82 Letter from Nicholson and Co. on subject of money due to John Hyde's estate and enquiring if balance might be paid to them on behalf of his sister and mother.

31.7.82 The brother of Miss Jackson, a pauper lunatic, appeared before the Guardians, but he declined to take her furniture and pay the value of it towards her maintenance at Wadsley. Resolved that they be sold.

16.10.82 In the case of E. Burdett, a girl gone to service. It was arranged that her wages be 1s a week for the first twelve months and that Mr Dawson the relieving officer provide her with clothes.

18.12.82 Resolved that William Burns be requested to attend the Guardians this day next month as to his brother Thomas Burns being sent to an orphan home in Sheffield through the influence of Revd Thomas Eyre.

29.1.83 Clerk reported Miss Robinson had called upon him respecting Ellen Bailey aged fifteen wishing, if possible, to take her to The Girls Friendly Society Lodge and asking the Guardians for an allowance. Resolved as she was an able-bodied girl that no relief be given.

13.2.83 Resolved the master give bedding to Ann Knapton.

26.3.83 Clerk reported John Barratt and Mary Crabtree are dead at Wadsley.

28.5.83 Mrs Norbrook applied to the Guardians for a reduction of the amount hitherto paid by her towards her daughter's maintenance in Wadsley Asylum. Resolved the Guardians refuse to alter this order and insist on her being proceeded against for the arrears, if not paid.

11.6.83 On the application of Mrs Swallow for Jane Lockwood to go and reside with her, it was resolved that the application be refused. Lydia Foer's application to go out be refused and the doctor declare her an imbecile.

18.6.83 Letter from Mr W.H. Sheldon informing the Guardians that the committee has decided to receive into the Wesleyan Children's Home at Belton two of the sons of the late Joe Barker and arrangements be made as soon as possible.

17.12.83 Letter from the Local Government Board that the Guardians had no power to prevent a parent from having the custody of his child and so it was ordered that Marie Cooper be given up to her mother.

10.3.84 Arthur Blacker, who was sent out under the Boarding Out Order: his mother now wishes for his restoration. Resolved that he be returned to the workhouse and then to be given up to his mother and to be clothed in the same clothing as he entered the workhouse. Mrs Bywater of 101½ Darwin Street, Birmingham wishing a girl in the workhouse called Fanny Robinson to be taken out. Resolved that enquiries be made at Birmingham, and, if satisfactory, that she be allowed to go.

10.5.84 Arnold Walker Wood (aged ten) and Annie Wood (aged four) be given the sum, not to exceed £10 each, to emigrate to California. Fred English of Maltby going to the Orphanage of Pity at Warminster.

17.11.84 Read letter from Mr C. Bellamy complaining of a pauper named Stevenson in receipt of relief which is not a deserving case. Resolved that Mr Dawson investigate the matter.

5.1.85 The clerk produced reports from the boarded out children Dickons, Walker, Smith, Crossley, Ward and Foote and each was very favourable.

6.7.85 Mary Anne Kennedy, daughter of Michael and Sarah Kennedy of 28 Regent Street, Wilton Gardens, Rotherham, who is an inmate at the Royal Albert Asylum, Lancaster, have one month's holiday.

3.8.85 Clerk read letter from Dr Hardwick as to William Symonds, who had been sent to the workhouse through destitution and had attempted to commit suicide, suggesting that he stay for a while, so he could be watched.

14.8.85 The sub-committee reported that a pauper inmate with four children named Priscilla Smith will take over the duties of caretaker as she constantly helped Miss Thornton. Resolved that she take over the duties for the time being. The arrangement to be supervised by the matron.

24.8.85 The master recorded that he had given in charge a vagrant named Thomas Curran for refusing to work and that the case would be heard on Friday next.

11.1.86 The clerk reported that he had searched through the Register of Shares of the North Central Wagon Co. as requested by the Guardians. A William Barber of 3 Saltergate, Chesterfield holding eight shares; second issue and two shares; fourth issue, the principal amounting to £121 15s at present price in the market. Resolved the clerk proceed against him for maintenance towards his father who is in the workhouse.

18.1.86 Letter from Dr Walker with received communication *re* Lunacy Commissioners regarding John Sellars, an idiot. Resolved the clerk to inform Dr Walker that, when the Guardians had the application before them, it was noted that the income of the family was more than £2 per week. Therefore it was not a pauper case and if the child were to be sent to an asylum it should be as a private patient.

1.9.90 Two boys named Curley to be detained in the house having been absent after school on several occasions.

13.10.90 Read letter from Doncaster Deaf and Blind school regarding Charles Simmons asking if the Guardians would pay 10s extra for instructions in turning and wood cutting for half a year, and also 15s in first instance for tools. Agreed.

10.11.90 Letter from Mr G.H. Smith, contractor for workhouse enlargement, asking the Guardians if he can use inmate called Bennett who he wishes to employ. Resolved the clerk to inform Mr Smith that if he wishes to employ Bennett he would have to leave the workhouse.

16.3.91 The clerk reported two letters respecting the removal to the workhouse of Ann Marriott who is charged with the murder of her infant child. The clerk reported that he had visited her in the workhouse and she was not in a fit state to be removed, but would be so in a very short time.

13.4.91 Letter from the master informing the Guardians that the woman Susannah Bailey, who has for several years acted as cook for the workhouse, was taking her discharge and advising that a paid cook is necessary as there is no other woman in the house equal to the work.

27.4.91 Resolved that Susannah Bailey have £2 of clothes on leaving the workhouse. (N.B. In the 1891 Census Susannah Bailey is 'aged sixty-two'. She was born at Greasebrough and is labelled 'imbecile'.)

6.7.91 Martha Richardson be allowed to go out to service to Mrs Hutchinson of 30 Ashwood Road, Parkgate subject to a month's trial. (N.B. In the 1891 Census Martha is a widow aged sixty-two, born in Carlisle.)

6.7.91 The law to prosecute in bastardy case of Dora Pinder and pay costs of same.

20.7.91 Letter received from, Joseph Taylor Ward of 15 Swinton Wharf, asking the Guardians for leave of absence for his daughter Charlotte Ann Ward (imbecile) for one week. Not granted.

21.12.91 Letter from Miss M. E. Arlidge informing the Guardians that £12 maintenance of Maud and Florence Tradewell in due to be paid and also stating that Maud, the elder girl, is now able to go out to a situation, and she had done well whilst in the orphanage and also that of her sister.

18.1.92 Clerk to send account to George Gummer for maintenance and nursing of a girl Nicklin whilst in workhouse suffering from scarlet fever and who was previously in service of George Gummer.

18.1.91 Resolved the boy Gray, now in the workhouse, be allowed to go and live with his aunt.

1.2.92 The girl Emily Waddington, an inmate of the workhouse who has on several occasions been sent out to service and returned for being disorderly, be sent to St Josephs Home at Sheffield. She be received into the school as a voluntary case, the Guardians paying 4s a week and material for five dresses in the year.

14.3.92 Resolved that Arthur Woolnough, thirteen, Ellen, eight, Marion, six, and Mary, three, having been deserted by their parents, be under the control of the Guardians (in the case of the boys to sixteen years and the girls eighteen years, pursuant to the Poor Law Act 1889).

28.3.92 James Tracy absconded in workhouse clothing. Clerk reported he had brought him before Mr Neill who remanded him till Thursday. The master stated the suit was worth 35s. Resolved the clerk, the master and Dobson attend the bench on Thursday. The boy Tracy had 12s on him.

12.9.92 On the application of Mr J. Charlton, blacksmith of Thorpe Hesley, it is resolved that the boy William Tracy be sent to him for a month on trial. (N.B. William Tracy in 1891 census is aged thirteen and listed as born at Rotherham.)

27.2.93 The clerk read the correspondence between himself and Messrs Saunders, Nicholson and Reedes in reference to the claim for maintenance of Betsy Jane Sayles, a pauper lunatic at Wadsley, informing the Guardians that she has inherited £56 6s 9d under the will of Mrs Harriett Sayles, deceased. The clerk received the money and handed over to the Guardians' collector.

21.4.93 The clerk stated that at the last meeting he was instructed to obtain a medical report as to the lad James Taylor suffering from chronic inflammation of the eyelids. It was resolved to get the boy examined by Dr Snell either at Rotherham or at Sheffield.

5.6.93 Letter from E. Piggott, clerk to the visiting justices at Wadsley Asylum, informing the Guardians that Jonathon France was admitted on the 8 June 1892 and was a suitable case to be returned if workhouse accommodation could be found for him (and also of Emily T. Kimber, aged eighteen, admitted 24 April 1893, owing to pressure on the female side). The medical superintendent would be glad for her to be returned if arrangements could be made to receive her back to the workhouse.

5.6.93 The master reported the sum of 8s found upon Peter Murphy. Resolved that the money be paid into bank to the credit of the union.

17.7.93 Read letter from the Superintendent for the Blind School at Liverpool with regard to John James Stretton and Florence Muscroft which states the pupils have nowhere to go during the summer holidays (from 31 July 1893 to 1 September 1893). Wishing to know if the Guardians will allow a sum not exceeding 10s 6d weekly in addition to contributions for educational expenses to enable the cases to be boarded out or sent to a convalescent home. The clerk stated that with regard to Muscroft, her mother had taken her, and with regard to Stretton, six months' notice be given to remove him from the school.

14.8.93 On Wednesday 9th, the deputation visited the Wadsley Asylum and had every lunatic before them from Rotherham (with the one exception of Emma Lambert, who was very bad in bed). Resolved if Emma Cashmere's husband will look after her and the wife of Matthew Straw, Dr Kay thinks they may be discharged. As to the boy John Peter Conroy, who was committed by the magistrate on 10 August to Wadsley, Dr Kay having confirmed by telephone that they could not take him, and the Guardians having no accommodation at Rotherham, the Guardians directed Mr Dawson to take him to the asylum.

25.9.93 Read letter from the Local Government Board stating the medical officer had informed them that Betsy Pashley, an imbecile inmate, had died suddenly on the 12th. They are requesting to be informed of the results of the inquest held on the body of the deceased. The clerk stated the master had handed over to him a letter from Mr Richard Walker of Silkstone Common near Barnsley asking if he be allowed to keep the boy Bennett another month on trial, which was granted.

9.10.93 The master reported that Thomas Connor, Thomas Lark and John Bee absconded in workhouse clothing and warrants to be taken out. Letter from the master reporting a slight fire which had broken out on Monday morning but was put out before doing much damage. The man suspected is Charles Smith. He enclosed a statement of evidence he had taken down from some of the inmates. The clerk read the statement and it was agreed not to prosecute.

15.12.93 Mr Savage of Wood Lane, Treeton applied to take the two brothers named Hancock out of the workhouse to live with him and asked for the usual scale for the youngest boy. Resolved that boys are allowed to go, and that 3s weekly and 5s ¼d for clothing be allowed for the youngest boy under the boarding out scheme. They to go for a month on trial.

15.1.94 Letter from the Superintendent of St Josephs Home requested he be furnished with one serge and one cotton dress for Emily Waddington for this year. Master instructed to supply the items. It was reported that Mr Twigg had attended the court this morning to give evidence in the case of the man Hannay whose wife and family had been in the workhouse for many months chargeable to the union, their costs amounting to £64 2s 6d. The magistrate had sent him to prison for three months with hard labour.

12.2.94 With regard to Mr Hannay, it was resolved that the sum of £2 reward be given to Mrs McGee, No. 3 Court, No. 6 House, Steel House Lane, Sheffield for laying the information leading to his arrest. 5s found on inmate Bernard Green, paid into the bank.

9.4.94 Letter from Wadsley *re* Charles Brodie Searle, admitted on 4.11.93, stating that the patient can be discharged on trial if he has any friends who can take care of him. The clerk reported that on receipt of the letter he had written a letter to Miss Searle of Cleethorpes, his sister, asking if she could take charge of him, but up to the present no reply. He was discharged 'to friends'.

7.5.94 The master reported that he had found 10s on the man Linney. It was resolved that the master pay it into the bank for pauper maintenance. The master reported 5d found on the woman Soakill and 1s 11d on the man Cushworth. The master was instructed to hand the money over on discharge.

16.7.94 Special spectacles be ordered for Peter Murphy, inmate, who is attending Sheffield Infirmary for the treatment of his eye.

13.8.94 On the application of Mrs P. Yalls of Eastwood Farm Cottage, Rotherham to adopt the young child named Hayes. Resolved take the child to the master to supply all the necessary clothes. Clerk reported Emma Cashmere, Emily Justice and Harriet Hawksworth had been received in the workhouse for one month.

10.9.94 The clerk reported that he had taken down the particulars of the woman Day relative to the case of Henry Day who had died before the arrival of Dr Branson. The statement to be sent to the Local Government Board.

5.11.94 It being reported that Charles Brodie Searle is dead.

14.1.95 Resolved the clerk write to Holyhead union *re* John Jones, a non-settled pauper there, and also Barnsley union *re* the case of Henry Barker and bring reports to the next board meeting. Ellen Griffiths, child inmate of the workhouse, being sent to Headingly Home for Waifs and Strays and asking sanction of the Local Government Board as the Home is uncertified.

28.1.95 Application received from uncle of three children of Mark Hudson who is now in Wadsley Asylum. Resolved the master visits the uncle and makes enquiries and if satisfied he allows the applicants to have the children. Henry Barton, aged eighty-three, in receipt of 6s weekly, and John Jones, aged eighty-seven, receiving 6s 6d weekly in out relief, was more than would be paid here. The clerk to write and ask if the old people were able to be removed, and if so send a medical order stating such. The Local Government Board had received from the medical officer, Dr Robinson, a report about the sudden death on 11th and 14th of inmates named Catherine Haley and Michael O'Brien. Details of the inquest to be reported to them. Clerk to write to the Governor of York prison and inform him that Emily Anson, wife of Albert Anson, is at present charged to the parish. She is unable to give the charge to which he was held and to write for information.

25.2.95 The Local Government Board to sanction 4s per week relief at Headingly so long as Ellen Griffiths is maintained there. The master is in communication with the matron of the home for the admission of the child.

11.3.95 The clerk read the following report made by the medical officer in his own book on the 8 March 1895: 'I have examined William Dodson as to his mental condition. I find him deficient mentally and that if he was sent to the Royal Albert Asylum there would be a good prospect of his being taught some trade so that ultimately he might earn his own living. Signed – Alfred Robinson MD'. Ellen Griffiths, cost of outfit of £3, to be paid by the Guardians.

6.5.95 Letter from Dr Weatherbe regarding special fee for attending upon Elizabeth Harrison, a very difficult case of childbirth with a deformed and contracted pelvis and that after trying unsuccessfully several methods of delivery was obliged to call in assistance and that it had been decided that the operation cranectomy was necessary and which had been successfully performed. Five guineas to be paid. Recommendation of the relief committee that two children named Merrick be sent to Headingly Home at 4s week maintenance.

3.6.95 Letter received from Headingly Home asking for £1 each for outfits for Merricks. Agreed.

15.7.95 Letter from the Medical Superintendent of Wadsley *re* Mildred Hall, aged six years, admitted at the asylum on 1 July 1895, asking to remove her to her proper union workhouse as being the proper place for such cases. The clerk to write to Dr Kay saying the Guardians are at present considering the desirability for providing separate accommodation and are in communication with the clerk of the peace at Wakefield on the subject.

29.7.95 Read letter from the honourable secretary of Sheffield Orphan Homes dated 20th respecting the case of George Walker, a boy at present in said institution, stating that a Mrs Dukenfield of Mill Yard, Kilnhurst, his grandmother, was willing to take him out of the house to reside with her. The clerk was instructed to write and say the Guardians have nothing to do with the matter.

26.8.95 Letter from the Local Government Board *re* report from the medical officer of the workhouse stating that an inmate named Olive Abdellah had died from being accidentally burnt and asking report of the inquest and full particulars.

23.9.95 Read letter from Mary Hazeldine of 95 Masbrough Street dated the 19th offering to adopt Beatrice Bagnall, now an inmate at the workhouse. The child should go to the home for a month's trial.

8.8.99 Letter from Hemsworth Union *re* John Webb, a pauper lunatic, admitting the settlement and stating the asylum authorities had been written to transfer costs of maintenance accordingly.

21.8.99 Letter from Mr Hickmott stating he had prosecuted the woman Margaret Godfrey for disobeying orders and wilful damage. She had been convicted and sentenced to 14 days imprisonment. Also in the case of Becky Moor for stealing a postal order, value 10s 6d, the property of the master. She had been convicted and committed to prison for three months with hard labour.

4.9.99 Read letter from the medical superintendent at Wadsley *re* Robert Huntingdon (Rotherham Bob), a pauper lunatic, stating that the asylum is very overcrowded at present and unless various Guardians are willing to assist them by taking a few of the more manageable and less dangerous patients, he feels it will be necessary to refuse admission to recent cases. He pointed out that cases sent to the workhouse still need care and supervision. The Guardians decided that nothing more could be done in the matter. Letter from the Local Government Board *re* the proposal of the Guardians to send Emily Bower to the Home for the Learning of Girls of Feeble Minds at Morpeth and the said house at Bow Villa, Morpeth has been certified by the Local Government Board and have fixed £15 12s per annum maximum as reasonable expenses for maintenance, clothing and education of each pauper sent. Received an application of Mr Twigg to sell furniture etc belonging to a pauper lunatic named Alice Foster. Agreed.

18.9.99 In the case of Robert Huntingdon (Rotherham Bob) at Wadsley, the medical superintendent stated that he is in a fit state to be returned to the workhouse.

2.10.99 Letter from Mr Hickmott stating that in the case of Charles Small who had deserted his family, the man had been convicted and committed to prison for two months with hard labour.

30.10.99 Resolved in the case of John Sugden suffering from rheumatism that he be sent to Buxton Baths. Admission £2 12s 6d.

13.11.99 Read letter from H. Hickmott *re* magistrate's order of 3s in the bastardy case of Kingswood and Thompson, to be paid until the child is fourteen years of age.

27.11.99 With regard to the deputation to the Royal Albert Idiot Asylum, Lancashire Mary E. Kennedy, Edwin Cheeseman and John Gleeson be removed as recommended in due course. The clerk to make arrangements.

11.12.99 Clerk read letter from Messrs Dixon and Horne (Asylum Department) acknowledging receipt of resolution passed by this Board of Guardians as to the case of William Casey and stating that medical superintendent was perfectly correct in refusing admission of the lunatic in question by virtue of the Register of Commission under Section 275 of the Lunacy Act 1890 and further stating that it is the duty of the Guardians to provide proper isolation and care of the patients. Letter from the Royal Albert *re* discharge of Mary E. Kennedy, Edwin Cheeseman and John Gleeson and stating the Guardians had better also apply for the discharge of Edgar Bray, Emily Lewis and John W. Dickenson who are not likely to do much good at the institution. Resolved that only the three original inmates to be removed. Letter from Mr Hickmott attended court *re* Joseph and Maurice Hobson in support of a summons against them for maintenance of their mother and an order to contribute 1s 6d each weekly had been made. In the case of Rocket and Jackson an order had been made of 3s weekly until the child is sixteen years.

23.12.99 Read letter from Mr Hockmott: he had attended court *re* Ogden desertion case but offered no evidence on the grounds that since her husband had left she had been living in adultery – which she admitted – and as a consequence the prisoner was discharged. The settlement of Anne Shelton at present at Wadsley were admitted by Barnsley union and case transferred accordingly

8.1.00 A letter addressed to Mr Twigg was read stating that he had found a man named Pilgrim and four children residing at 24 Wilton Lane, suffering from typhoid fever and appearing to be entirely without means. In consequence of the borough having no provision for isolating such cases the clerk to write to the borough and lay the matter before them.

22.1.00 Ernest Richards for neglecting to obey summons. The magistrates ordered to pay off arrears at 1s 6d a week as well as 2s 6d a week. A man named William Mason prosecuted under Vagrancy Act for neglecting to maintain his wife, convicted and committed to prison for one calendar month. Regarding the case of typhoid fever at Wilton Lane, Mr Twigg asked the doctor to see the cases which he had and recommended they be isolated. He had been in contact with the master who sent a nurse down in a cab to take charge of the patients. Mr Pilgrim said they were not paupers and refused to go to the workhouse. They had their own doctor and he would attend to them. Mr Twigg reported the man had since died leaving seven children and his wife who had been compelled to apply for relief. In consequence of this he had completed a report which would be sent to the Local Government Board.

5.2.00 The Local Government Board noted that amongst admittance to the workhouse isolation hospital was that of Minnie Taylor, aged seven, suffering from enteric fever, who died the following day. The board wished to see a copy of the request as to why she was admitted. The clerk had the copy of the certificate, which would be sent to the Local Government Board. Letter from Mr Hickmott regarding the man Emery who was convicted and ordered to pay 7s per week for maintenance of his wife.

19.2.00 The clerk reported the settlement of Sarah Ann Marsh, a pauper lunatic chargeable to Chesterfield, who had been transferred.

5.3.00 The clerk reported that he had been in touch with the MP for Rotherham and the Commissioner of Chelsea Hospital with regard to a pension in the case of a man named Yardley, an old soldier, who had been granted out relief temporarily and was now ill and totally incapacitated. It is likely the man will receive the special campaign pension of 9d per day. The matter to be left in the hands of the clerk. The clerk reported that in the accounts of Dr Robinson he had charged 31s 6d for chloroform, which needed the sanction of the Local Government Board, for George Baker, aged fifty-three years, who was admitted to the workhouse on the 11 December 1899 suffering from a dislocation of the shoulder.

19.3.00 Letter from the Local Government Board *re* the medical officer's certificate which had been sent to them regarding Minnie Taylor who, suffering from typhoid fever, was brought into the workhouse isolation hospital. The workhouse hospital is intended solely for destitute persons. Guardians are not empowered to admit non-pauper cases nor to relieve the Sanitary Authority from the duty of providing for accommodation such cases. The hospital accommodation should be provided by the Sanitary Authority. The Guardians should enter into an agreement for the maintenance on such terms as mutually agreed upon.

2.4.00 The clerk reported two cases chargeable to the workhouse, namely Thomas Lee of Aston under Lyme and John Fletcher and family of Halifax. Both unions had refused settlement without a magistrate's order. The clerk to obtain the magistrate's order. An application of Mr Wright be allowed to take his brother, an inmate certified as an imbecile, out of the workhouse to live with him. Agreed.

24.6.00 The Royal Hospital Chelsea regarding Yardley, late of the Grenadier Guards: in consideration of former war service, they had awarded him a special compassionate campaign pension at 9d a day from 1 April 1900. Yardley died on 29 April, the clerk to inform them. Emma Whelan, a pauper patient discharged from Devonshire Hospital, Buxton, has improved.

29.10.00 The deputation to Lancaster Idiot Asylum to see cases chargeable to the union reported: five cases which could be brought back to the workhouse, namely William Dodson, Tom Hattersley, Samuel Littlewood, C.E. Hincliffe and J.M. Dickenson. Two remaining cases, Emily Lewis and Edgar Bray, remain. The clerk to write to say the cases will be removed at the end of the quarter year. The clerk reported four children named Walker suffering from scarlet fever, paupers who had been admitted to the Borough Isolation Hospital (there being no provision for isolation at the workhouse). Letter from the town clerk asking for two guineas each per week for maintenance. The Guardians feel the two guineas each a heavy charge. A committee to be deputised to attend the town clerk and discuss.

10.12.00 Letter from Messrs Saunders and Nicholson, clerks to Wath District Council, enclosing letter from Oxley and Coward regarding the maintenance of Thomas Kitchen and his three children who were sent to Hoober Hospital in the rural district with typhoid. The account amounted to £54 5s 9d. Agreed to bring it to the Rural District Council meeting this afternoon.

4.2.01 Letter from Wadsley regarding Charles Albert Stone and John Peter Conroy, who have been removed to Stanley Hall, a part of Wakefield Asylum, with special accommodation for idiot children.

With regard to the pauper named Kitchen removed from Wath district to Hoober Hospital, a cheque for £27 2s 11d to be paid by the Guardians as a more reasonable sum than £54 5s 9d.

18.2.01 The clerk reported Mr Cobban is in court this morning with reference to the case named Jeremiah Cod who had tried to hang himself after being turned down by Mr Cobban for out relief. The report read from Mr Cobban. The Guardians say no blame was to be attached to him and he had done his duty.

4.3.01 Letter from the Admiralty dated the 28th respecting a pensioner named Norbury and asking for further information.

18.3.01 Letter from Wadsley regarding William John Coulsey Bray and Tom Hattersley, who had been removed from Wadsley to Stanley Hall.

13.5.01 Dr Robinson gave a recommendation for Buxton Baths in the case of Annie Gabriel, suffering from rheumatism.

10.6.01 The clerk reported that he had received an order to admit Emily Heeds into the Chesterfield union workhouse. The order was given to the master, who was removing the case today. The clerk reported that he had written to the Local Government Board regarding three orphan children named Butts in Swinton parish being allowed relief. It was agreed they go to live with their elder sister, who is clean, respectable and deserving woman, and had received a reply giving their sanction on condition that the Boarding Out of Children with the Various Unions Order of 1889 be strictly adhered to.

6.8.01 Mr Jeffrey had attended the court regarding David Street of Swinton who had deserted his wife and family, leaving them chargeable to this union. The magistrate sentenced him to two months' imprisonment.

19.8.01 The clerk produced a magistrate's order which had been obtained for Richard Lambert of Wath, whose daughter was a pauper lunatic at Wadsley, having ascertained that the latter had a sum of money in Post Office Savings Bank and which sum or sums must now be set apart towards the cost of maintenance. The clerk undertook to hand the order to Mr Lambert.

16.9.01 The deputation to Birkenhead was well satisfied with everything they saw (on the training ship *Indefatigable*) and the three boys, Halswell, Vernon and South, be sent as soon as possible. Resolved that the boy John Robey Johnson be allowed to go to Mr Trickett of Dalton for a month's trial. The Guardians decided not to allow the girl Lily Maddison, aged twelve and a half, to be taken out by her aunt Mrs Robinson, the surroundings of her proposed home being unsatisfactory.

14.10.01 Richard Lambert of Wath, a lunatic chargeable to the workhouse: the money in the Post Office Savings Bank had been procured. Fulford, a deserter whose wife was chargeable to the workhouse: the master reported that she had taken her discharge.

25.10.01 A reward of two guineas paid to police officer Green in respect of the arrest of the man named Slack for desertion; Slack had subsequently been committed to prison for three months.

20.1.02 A cheque of four guineas drawn in favour of the chief constable, being a reward of two guineas each, in the case of Dyson and Thacker who had deserted their families. An inmate named Mills appeared before the Guardians relative to his child who had been for the last three years with Mr and Mrs Whitely and who was wishful to have possession of his child. It was reported that the child had an exceedingly good home and the Guardians expressed themselves not in favour of the move. It was resolved that the matter be left in the hands of the master and that before next board day the medical officer give a medical report on the man Mills' physical fitness for employment. A Mr Willie Jenkins and his wife of 2 Douglas Street, Parkgate appeared before the board and asked to be allowed to take out the illegitimate child belonging to Beatrice Lee alias Hawkins, a blind woman in the workhouse. In answer to the chair Jenkins promised to take great care of the child. The blind woman attended before the board and gave her consent to the child being taken out and adopted by Jenkins and his wife. In the case of Arthur Myers, the master to get a report from the medical officer *re* his physical fitness for employment.

3.3.02 Letter from the clerk of the School Board at Rawmarsh regarding the boy Dickenson who was removed to the Royal Albert Asylum. He is removed from there because he was not making any progress.

26.5.02 That two cases still at the Royal Albert, Edgar Bray and Emily Lewis, be returned back to the workhouse.

9.6.02 Letter from Mr Bray regarding his son and asking that he be allowed to stay at the Royal Albert. Resolves that the clerk write to the secretary of the asylum and make enquiries as to his progress, what he is engaged in at the moment and any general information. A pauper, Eliza Shawcroft, was due to be transferred from Rotherham to Chapel en le Frith, but was put off due to a case of smallpox there. A cheque for two guineas paid for the apprehension of James Mann for the desertion of his wife and three children.

7.7.02 Letter from the union clerk of Chapel en le Frith regarding their workhouse: it is now free from smallpox, and Eliza Shawcroft can go now. Sent the latter to Mr Jeffreys who said the woman refused to be moved.

2.7.02 Letter from the secretary of the Royal Albert *re* Albert Bray. The clerk was asked to readmit him as soon as possible. Letter from Wadsley regarding Douglas Guest aged seven who was admitted on 4 July 1902 and had been sent to Stanley Hall, an asylum especially for children.

1.9.02 The master reported the baker Mr McClure had become insane and moved to Wadsley, the form of insanity being religious mania. It was carried unanimously that the Guardians pay a part of his wages – namely 10s a week – for one month. At the end of the month the asylum authorities to be asked for a report as to probable date of his recovery if possible. The inmate Henry Mann, who had since Mr McClure's incapacity performed the baking at the workhouse, be appointed baker pro tem and he to be remunerated at 2s 6d per week. The master is authorised to engage further help in the bake house should the occasion arise. The clerk reported the indenture of apprenticeship between the Guardians, Vincent Brown and Mr William Clark, joiners of Rawmarsh Hill, be signed by the chair as both the latter had signed it.

27.10.02 A report from the captain superintendent of the training ship *Indefatigable* regarding the two boys there from the union workhouse named South and Vernon was read and considered satisfactory. The report stated that they still had vacancies on the ship, and was referred to the house committee.

8.12.02 With reference to the boy Shaw who was selected to the Guardians to be sent to the training ship *Indefatigable*, it was agreed not to send him as his aunt had agreed to take him out of the house.

22.12.02 Stanley Hall Asylum has no vacancies for a youth named Clarke to go. Letter from Dr Weatherbe giving an explanation of the case of Slattery who was sent into the workhouse with smallpox.

Bibliography

Primary Sources

The Board of Guardians' minute books
July 1837 – Oct 1843 (Oct 1843 – August 1848 missing)
Aug 1848 – Nov 1851
Nov 1851 – Feb 1855 (Feb 1855 – Oct 1859 missing)
Oct 1859 – Dec 1864
Dec 1864 – June 1869
June 1869 – Mar 1872
Mar 1872 – Dec 1874
Dec 1874 – Dec 1878 (Dec 1878 – Jan 1881 missing)
Jan 1881 – Sept 1883
Oct 1883 – Feb 1886 (Feb 1886 – April 1889 missing)
April 1889 – Dec 1891
Jan 1892 – Jan 1894
Jan 1894 – Oct 1895 (Oct 1895 – Jul 1899 missing)
Jul 1899 – April 1901
April 1901 – Dec 1902

Religious Creed Register 1884 - 1887
Religious Creed Register 1897 -1900
South Yorkshire Asylum for the West Riding in the County of York
Register of Pauper Patients
Census Returns
Workhouse Admissions Book

Secondary Sources

Crowther, M.A., *The Workhouse System 1834-1929: The History of an English Social Institution* (London, Methuen, 1983)
Driver. F. *Power and Pauperism: The Workhouse System 1834 – 1884* (Cambridge, New York, Melbourne, Madrid and Cape Town, Cambridge University Press, 2004)
Hey, D., *The Making of South Yorkshire* (Derbyshire, Moorland Publishing Co., 1979)
Longmate, N., *The Workhouse: A Social History* (London, Australia, New Zealand and South Africa, Pimlico, 2003)

The two maps reproduced in this book are reduced from the original maps:
Fig. 12 Reproduced from the Ordinance Survey Map Surveyed 1888 Scale 1:2,500 1st Edition Ref 289 -11 courtesy of RALS
Fig. 23 Reproduced from the Ordinance Survey Map Surveyed in 1888 Scale 1:500 Ref 289-11-17) also courtesy of RALS

Electronic Sources

The Andover Workhouse Scandal, Victorian Web, http://victorian web.org/history/poorlaw/andover.html
Gummer, G., 'Reminiscences of Rotherham', http://www.rotherhamweb.co.uk/h/gummer/index.htm
The Fareham Workhouse Scandal, http://www3.hants.gov.uk/museum/westbury-manor-museum/westbury-local-studies/fareham-workhouse.htm
Higginbotham, P. ,The Rotherham Workhouse, http://www.workhouses.org.uk
Hobbs, C., http://www.chrishobbs.com
Hull in Print (Hull City Council), http://static.hullcc.gov.uk/hullinprint/archive/augsep2001/no_place_like.html
The Martley Workhouse Scandal, http://archive.worcesternews.co.uk
Rivett, G. The Development of the London Hospital System, Poor Law Infirmaries, http://www.nhshistory.net/poor_law_infirmaries.htm
The Rotherham Website, http://www.rotherhamweb.co.uk
Victorian Web, http://www.victorianweb.org
1891 Census, Rotherham Union Workhouse, http://www.rotherhamweb.co.ul/h/twhouse.htm

Newspapers

RAMA – Rotherham and Masbrough Advertiser
RJ – Rotherham Journal